THE GOOD BUD GUIDE

PUBLISHED BY GREEN CANDY PRESS
San Francisco, CA

Copyright © 2005 Albie

1-931160-34-1

This book contains information about illegal substances, specifically the plant Cannabis Sativa and its derivative products. Green Candy Press would like to emphasize that Cannabis is a controlled substance in North America and throughout much of the world. As such, the use and cultivation of cannabis can carry heavy penalties that may threaten an individual's liberty and livelihood.

The aim of the Publisher is to educate and entertain. Whatever the Publisher's view on the validity of current legislation, we do not in any way condone the use of prohibited substances.

Printed in China
MASSIVELY DISTRIBUTED BY P.G.W.

THE GOOD BUD GUIDE

by Albie

GREEN CANDY PRESS

CONTENTS

KEY | GROW ROOM NOTES + | ➕

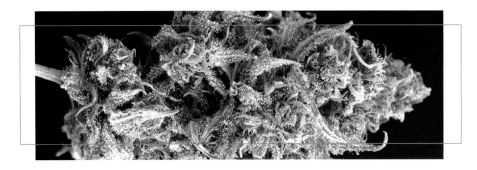

VARIETIES TEXT

FLOWER PERIOD: 56-63 days
APPROX. FINISHED ON-SET HEIGHT: 100%
MAXIMUM RELATIVE HUMIDITY: 65%

MAXIMUM TDS / EC: 1.4 / CF: 14 / PPM: 980
3 x 400 WATT x 25cm POT / YIELD = 90gms+

The "at-a-glance" info box that starts each variety is as follows:

FLOWER PERIOD: 49-56 days

FLOWER PERIOD:

The first figure is the earliest, acceptable finish with the second figure being the premium finish.

APPROX. FINISHED ON-SET HEIGHT: 85-110%

APPROX. FINISHED ON-SET HEIGHT:

This is an approximation of the extra growth (%) made from point of onset inducement (12 hours cycle) until the start of the fourth week. Most varieties in this book had onset induced at approximately 50-60cm height.

MAXIMUM RELATIVE HUMIDITY: 70%

MAXIMUM RELATIVE HUMIDITY:

The levels quoted are what the plants' environment was recording through flowering cycle; it is very possible with certain strains to go higher than the quoted figure.

MAXIMUM TDS / EC: 1.4 / CF: 14 / PPM: 980

MAXIMUM TDS (TOTAL DISSOLVABLE SOLIDS):

You will require a meter to record feed strength in order to use this information. The feeds apply to Hydro A + B nutrients as the meter does not work with organics (see breakdown of organic feeds on page 5).

3 x 400 WATT x 25cm POT / YIELD = 85gms+

YIELD:

Referring to the two different light wattages used for this project, earlier models were grown as two rows of 6 plants in 25cm pots of coco-coir using three x 400 watt lights.

3 x 600 WATT x 25cm POT / YIELD = 140gms+

The later setup used three x 600 watt lights so yields are considerably different and cannot be compared. These figures under the circumstances can be increased, considerably in some setups.

MAXIMUM RESIN PRODUCTION AT 49 DAYS

MAXIMUM RESIN PRODUCTION AT 49 DAYS:

This refers to a few plants that produce excessive resin at start of week seven regarding 7-8 week finishers.

MULTIPLE SINGLE STEM

This is regarding growers, commercial or personal, that use high numbers of single stem plants as opposed to multi-limbed, large versions. An ideal hydroponic high-turnover setup would use a large Flood 'n' Drain tray (90cm square) setup for planting 32 stems, rooted in rockwool and laid in the tray half-filled with clay balls. Once plants are evenly spaced, cover rockwool base with clay balls and continue filling to within 2.5cm of top of tray. Position a 600-watt light 1 meter above plant tops, reducing height 10-15cm every four days to offset shock of high lumens till correct height is achieved. These cuttings must be taken from a mother plant in vegetation (18-24 hour) cycle to prevent lateral growth.

Alternatively, a heavy-duty version of the above setup is a very easy addition, and the resulting yields need to be experienced rather than read about to be believed. Purchase a reflector that allows a second bulb to be placed at the opposite end (bulbs are nose-to-nose). A second lamp holder and ballast would be required, adding as many watts to the existing setup as you like. A second 600-watt bulb will give 1200 watts, illuminating a 90 square centimeter area. Take time to supercrop each tray of stems; this couple of hours' work can return up to double the standard harvest.

The stems will be like celery sticks and not require the twisting method; preferably, just gently squeeze the stem between thumb and forefinger to hear a quiet crack—sometimes the crack can be felt—being careful to cease the squeeze immediately as the hurd cracks or gives. Be careful not to squash the stem or cause it to split, only the inner hurd needs damaging and this does not require much pressure.

Start at the base squeezing approximately every 2cm up the stem. This can be done just before on set or actually when on set is induced. Do not treat later than the start of the second week as this will interrupt the budding cycle. Of course, this can be utilized without the extra bulb, but when both are incorporated the sight can seriously damage your health.

This type of setup requires excellent air movement (not relaying to extraction) within the grow room. Recommendations are for a 48cm fan or two blowing air away between plant tops and bulbs, another 48cm pedestal fan on a table moving air between the tops of reflectors (light shades) and the ceiling of the room. The air movement will cause single stems to move constantly, stimulating extra root growth. Excellent reflection will play a central role in this setup's maximum yield potential as will experience and choice of plant.

THE PROJECT

The aim of this book is to give accurate, non-biased write-ups on a variety of plants. This being a self-funded project, no seed banks have been named and the strains discussed here were from seeds purchased from a UK-based seed distributor, who were extremely helpful and patient, with excellent stock availability. Friends also made purchases that helped increase the number of strains for this book. Neither seed banks nor any other companies were involved with this project regarding information *i.e.*, Sativa or Indica parentage.

I have found great variation in a packet of ten seeds in most varieties, and that being the case, some specifications of a plant may not have the same format as independent research provided, yet the aroma, flavor and effect are spot-on. For example (this variation affects all the strains in this book and I am simply picking two at random) Leda Uno has two phenotypes, one short and chunky, the other tall and lean, the latter being the seed bank's preferred choice. The Ultimate Indica is described as a short bushy heavy yielder, yet two of the females from the seed pack raced off when mature and developed even faster when onset induced. One Ultimate Indica that is the book model is the ideal format, while the other two reached almost two meters!

The flip side to varying phenotypes for the grower would be this: as long as you get enough females to select from, you can have the format that best suits your growing environment. If you do not strike high on females you could be left with an example that grows completely opposite to what you should have. Look for early telltale signs of a phenotype you are selecting, such as speed of growth, distance of nodal points, that can be identified before investing too much time into the wrong phenotype. I have remained objective as I see the varieties, but there will always be differences of opinion and that is necessary and productive.

The only problem I see currently is the duplication of strains named the same as the original that have problems right from the beginning, and this needs to be addressed.

I wanted to express the plants' aromas and flavors and help potential growers to appreciate these aspects. Flavors I have been enchanted with range

Organic Bubbleberry flowered for nine weeks.

Hydro Bubbleberry flowered for nine weeks. Courtesy of Smuttley

from blueberry yogurt, lemon meringue, mango, orange, cream soda (root beer) to cleaning fluid, hashy-fuel, old cheese, noodle, beef casserole/broth, pepper to sandalwood, floral and musk. To condition your palate to these flavors can take some practice.

Try working with established flavors that you can practice identifying, capturing those quintessential aromas and tastes that reveal a particular strain's unique identity. Eliminating one of the senses, such as sight, helps to sharpen the remaining senses. Try candlelight or blindfold for research.

For the strains grown in this project, I chose coco-coir out of curiosity and was very impressed with its performance. I selected a hydro-based nutrient for the grow cycle, and A+B coco-coir feed to ensure, through the early vegetation stage, the plants received a perfect diet for good strong growth. After the first week of onset passed a selection of off-the-shelf ready-made organic nutrients were combined for the flowering mix per 10 liters of water:

OZI MAGIC MONSTER BUD	20 mls per 10 litres
OZI TONIC	20 mls per 10 litres
BUD GROW	20 mls per 10 litres
NATRAKELP	20 mls per 10 litres
SUPERTHRIVE (NON-ORGANIC)	2 mls per 10 litres
NATURESOWN SUPER BLOOM	20 mls per 10 litres
BIO-BUGS OR	1 tsp per 50 litres
CANNA ZYM	40 mls per 10 litres

PH was set to 6.0-6.4 and every third feed I flushed with water and dissolved a level teaspoon of Bio-Bugs. The above mix allows many of the outdoor characteristics of leaves fading and an array of colors are exhibited from the buds when removed from the grow room and placed under natural light. The finished produce is as close to outdoor herb as is possible to achieve, although still a way behind. For indoor gardens, organic nutrients produce herb with excellent flavor, clarity of aroma and a very impressive high. Coco hydro feeds have Bloom A+B but most plants remain a lush green throughout flowering with little fade off. When using A+B grow/flower nutrients, the finished product is excellent considering it is inexpensive, with an easy delivery; incorporating regular flushing with a two week flush to finish it produces a very clean, impressive product.

Outdoor plants are the epitome of this industry. You cannot put a wattage on sunlight, along with the many other attributes the sun's light brings. Indoor gardens are a copy of the real thing; an extremely good copy, which allows for growing all year round as well as secrecy. Outdoors organic is unquestionably superior on every level but many growers do not have the luxury of outdoor growing so indoor gardening is the next best thing, along with continuous production, which outdoors/greenhouse can also have by using a small room/cupboard with a light in it to grow cuttings taken from a mother one week into onset, producing a multi-limbed, open format from the start. When the cuttings reach the grower's required height, replant in greenhouse or outdoor plot. No matter what time of the year, the light hours outdoors are always less than the 18 hour vegetative cycle the cuttings receive artificially and most strains will revert to onset (flowering cycle) immediately.

The industry has done unbelievable work to bring gardens indoors and recreate a near to natural environment for successful growing. Still, plants grown correctly outdoors in a good environment will be nothing less than perfect examples of color, aroma and flavor with effects that go off the meter.

The feed applied to this crop was a Coco Hydroponic Nutrient A+B with a two week flowering booster addition through weeks five and six, flushing regularly and finishing with a two week flush. It produced an aromatic, flavorsome bounty of mixed varieties with a very potent effect.

FIRST EXPERIENCE

My curiosity to grow was aroused after a couple of trips to Amsterdam. Until then, like most people, I had been purchasing my herb since 1978. I spent my time there seeking as much knowledge as I could and also purchasing a recommended beginners' grow guide that I posted home as customs would have a field day with that one. Realizing I had to purchase two x 400 watt lights, I didn't know where to begin as this was 1991 and there were very few if any specific hydroponic outlets.

A garden weekly paper leaped out at me at the supermarket one day with an advert heading more eye catching than the title of the paper, which read *Grow Your Own.* I purchased it and there was the information I wanted, 250-watt, 400-watt, MH and HPS lighting for vegetables and flowers. My uncle had agreed to utilize one of his bedrooms, which had formerly been my cousin's— a real head himself.

We did it properly with pulleys for lights, raised floor for aeration and supported beams for the lights. For our first attempt, I used the seeds I had saved from past Thai deals. Many germinated and after sexing them I placed 16 females into 25cm pots, without a moment's thought or experience given to lighting factors; to a pair of first-timers 16 pots under two x 400 watt lights not only looked sufficiently lit, but we proceeded to place six more pots in there.

I allowed them to mature and proceeded to induce onset when most were approximately four feet tall. Over the next four weeks they touched the ceiling twice. We had to tie them down. My uncle kept saying "this can't be right." We waited nine weeks to reveal fingernail-sized buds, or trim was what we were left with, not knowing this strain flowers for 14-16 weeks and then doesn't yield heavy for indoors.

For our second attempt we purchased seeds from Amsterdam that were a Sativa/Indica cross. Again I allowed them to reach chest height before inducing onset and they also had to be tied down. There were 12 this time and halfway through flowering my uncle went on holidays for 5 weeks, the duration of the crop.

I looked after them full-time and these were looking much more like it. On the eighth week, I decided to feed them the nutrient three times, as up to then, it was one feed and the rest of the week was water, since we were using a crystal-based general horticulture feed that had a NPK reading on the grow of 35:10:10 and flower was 10:20:25. The purpose for the extra dosing was to get them bigger. Ignorance is bliss.

I walked in the room the day after the third feed and to my horror, they looked like they had been torched with a flame thrower. Not one escaped and my uncle on his return 'hit the ceiling' twice. These were dreadful experiences for us but we learned so much from them.

With patience and diligence, excellent results can be achieved, as reflected by this El Niño.

AAA

FLOWER PERIOD: 56-63 days
APPROX. FINISHED ON-SET HEIGHT: 50-75%
MAXIMUM RELATIVE HUMIDITY: 65%

MAXIMUM TDS / EC: 1.4 / CF: 14 / PPM: 980
3 x 400 WATT x 25cm POT YIELD = 90gms+

This is not the original AAA that Mr. J.K. writes of; this is a completely different strain using the same title rather confusingly, as this variety does deserve a name of its own. It's a big Indica, thick, dense and with closely staggered nodal points that ensure profuse lateral development later in life or if tipped, moving away from center, that open the structure up allowing light full access to all budding sites as they develop. The dark green leaves are extremely large and of a round serration, some tending to obstruct light to secondaries, so cutting blades width-ways removing 50% of the leaf allows light to reach hidden buds.

Tipping for large plant setups, allow AAA to reach 25-30cm to ensure a high number of laterals that facilitate in the excessive returns this plant is capable of. For a big plant, ensure AAA is of a good size, approximately 50-60cm height, before inducing onset. The surge of growth through the first four weeks of the 12-hour cycle will result with a finished sized plant that is approximately 50-70% bigger, i.e., if AAA is 50cm when onset is induced, it

The Notorious London Cabbie holds a AAA grown in a Dutch Pot hydro system. Photo Credit: NLC

will have a finished height of 75-85cm by the end of the fourth week of onset. In multiple single stem setups, AAA will require extra vegetation time; allow cuttings to reach 20-25cm before inducing onset for excessive colas by 63 days. Budding sites are at

'locking up' distance from the dirt up and using good reflection, the base nugs will have the density of primary buds.

Keep EC levels low, flushing weekly and ensuring a two week flush to finish for optimum results. Average mold resistance, tolerating relative humidity up to 70%, however the colas can get enormous (up to the size of a person's head, particularly in hydro setups), so if this figure cannot be reduced, observe for dying leaves and remove immediately for peace of mind. I would recommend keeping relative humidity below 65% and if possible a little lower.

Outdoor/greenhouse growers will require a mild to arid climate, the grower knowing best his own environment, but with an extended vegetation cycle and benefiting from tying down, this plant's returns should carry a health warning! Leave are plenty through growth/early budding cycles but tend to fade to the background as the colas develop their humungous size. Allowing plants to dry (for best results a four-week dry in the dark) before manicuring will dramatically reduce the amount of leaf removal as the resin coverage is very good, spilling onto the surrounding bud leaves.

AROMA, TASTE AND EFFECT

The bud has a strong pungent aroma, heavy, dank, peppery on the nose. The taste is hashy flavor, very pleasant and not complex. The effect is cerebral and uplifting, making it excellent after breakfast with a coffee. The duration ebbs away without notice, a real quality day smoke. Curing will add a smoothness and richness to the smoke and the effect becomes more sedative.

AFGHAN X SKUNK

FLOWER PERIOD: 56-63 days
APPROX. FINISHED ON-SET HEIGHT: 100-130%
MAXIMUM RELATIVE HUMIDITY: 80%

MAXIMUM TDS / EC: 1.4 / CF: 14 / PPM: 980
3 x 600 WATT x 25cm POT / YIELD = 150gms+

This variety is a yield-master of the highest quality bud. It roots from clone without a problem and grows at a fast pace producing staggered nodal points, ensuring a profuse development of laterals later in life or when tipped. Laterals develop close to the main stem growing vertically and parallel, producing a 'tower' format that does not open out making it ideal for close quarters growing. The leaves are predominately medium-sized with a liberal scattering of large fans, so there is no obstruction of light to buds.

A setup growing large indoor plants should tip at approximately 25-30cm allowing for a profuse development of laterals. Inducing onset at approximately 50-60cm+ will gain an extra 100-130% height. Tying down will allow Afghan x Skunk to reach full potential and return excessive yields, although development of budding sites is unaffected through onset—remaining closely staggered, locking up at the midway point of stems to produce typical Sativa length, Indica girth, resin dripping colas! In a multiple single stem setup Afghan x Skunk requires little vegetation time, allowing cutting to reach 15-20cm (depending on setup) before inducing onset for stunning returns. (Note that the phrase "depending on setup" in these listings refers to the vast diversity of variables in any given grow, e.g., medium, number of water deliveries, number and size of lights, and so on, which may affect the outcome.)

This plant has excellent resistance to mold, tolerating relative humidity of 80%. Keep EC levels low, flushing weekly, and allow a two-week flush to finish. Outdoor/greenhouse growers should have excellent results with extended vegetation cycle, tipping and tying, the potency of this strain grown outdoors would have to be treated very seriously indeed. The colas have a finished format resembling Skunk #1—locking budding sites spiraling up the stems until the slowing of growth through onset surge allows them to group crowdedly toward the tops like an inverted champagne bottle. When allowed to dry in the dark over four weeks, there is very little manicuring needed.

AROMA, TASTE AND EFFECT

This plant has a really strong, skunky hash fragrance. When jarred, opening the jar will immediately fill the room with a coffee skunk aroma, but when the bud is cut a strong aniseed fragrance is released with undertones of skunk. The taste is a smooth hash flavor with a hint of aniseed. The effect is sedative, heavy head, heavy body with no ceiling limit. Excellent for end of the day, evening and weekends. This is potent brew and cured, it is this industry's "Moonshine."

CURED BUD

CURED BUD/CLOSEUP

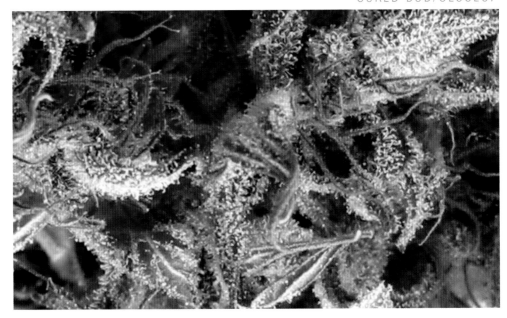

AMERICAN DREAM

FLOWER PERIOD: 49-56 days
APPROX. FINISHED ON-SET HEIGHT: 50-75%
MAXIMUM RELATIVE HUMIDITY: 70%

MAXIMUM TDS / EC: 1.4 / CF: 14 / PPM: 980
3 x 600 WATT x 25cm POT / YIELD = 130gms+

A slow-paced Indica that develops an abundance of nodal points that ensure a dense, compact structure of laterals when the plant matures or when tipped. For large plant setups, allow American Dream to reach approximately 25-30cm before tipping, to ensure a high number of laterals that move away from center very slowly with a profuse development of secondaries that give the format a very busy, congested look and do not open up until well mature. The plant has a large, dark green leaf format that in some cases may require cutting width-ways across the leaf to remove 50% and expose hidden budding sites to the light.

In large plant setups, allow American Dream to reach 50-60cm before inducing onset as an overall gain of approximately 50-75% can be expected. Keep EC levels low and flush frequently, ensuring a two-week flush to finish. Multiple single stem setups would need a longer vegetation time due to slow pace of growth even through onset allowing cutting to reach approximately 20-25cm before inducing onset.

Outdoor/greenhouse growers will reap excessive returns, with the extended vegetation cycle and good mold resistance, although they will need to observe cola/bud development nearing finish if unexpected, prolonged wet cycle occurs, although short flowering time should keep it ahead of seasonal change. This is an ideal variety where gardens suffer height restrictions, also exceptional in setups requiring excessive returns using fewer plants. The colas and buds have a good, finished look to them at 49 days; if allowed to run till 56 days, there is a noticeable difference in size and resin coverage, the buds looking like sparkling pinecones of similar size and density. A few wispy leaves extend from high calyx to leaf buds, making manicuring after drying very quick, and there's little scent through flowering cycle unless disturbed. American Dream is a mega-yielder in any setup, building dense, resin-laden buds from the dirt up (good reflection will govern this response) excessively and consistently. What a masterpiece!

AROMA, TASTE AND EFFECT

The aroma, when the plant is cut, is a citrus-lime eruption and the mouth responds. The flavor transitions to taste well; like a lime cordial it leaves the palate with a very refreshed feeling. The effect fuzzies thoughts very quickly, causing eyelids to feel heavy. It is a very sedative hit of the highest quality coming over the top of many other strains you may have indulged in the same session. Excellent for winding down with at the end of the day or before bed. The effect has a very long duration if required, making it ideal if the situation of long breaks between tokes arises.

CURED BUD

CURED BUD/CLOSEUP

BIG BUD

FLOWER PERIOD: 56-63 days
APPROX. FINISHED ON-SET HEIGHT: 60-85%
MAXIMUM RELATIVE HUMIDITY: 65%

MAXIMUM TDS / EC: 1.4 / CF: 14 / PPM: 980
3 x 400 WATT x 25cm POT / YIELD = 95gms+

A classic, well-established strain that always returns exceptional yields, Big Bud is a slow grower with closely staggered nodal points ensuring prolific lateral growth later in life or if tipped. A knuckle develops where the lateral grows off the main stem to help support the impressive buds and colas this variety yields. For big indoor plants, tip at approximately 25-30cm to facilitate a high number of laterals that slowly move away from center although the profuse secondary development gives Big Bud a very busy, congested appearance. Alternatively, take a cutting from a mother one week into onset as this will engage lateral development immediately after rooting, giving Big Bud a very advanced structure at such an early stage. Budding sites are compact and congested with some heads hidden by the large, round serrated leaves that may require a 50% removal of offending leaf blades.

As a multiple single stem candidate this variety excels, capable of producing oversized colas, although longer vegetation time would be required, inducing onset at approximately 20-25cm. The wrong phenotype selection can see a prolific surge of growth but the correct choice has Big Bud modestly responding to onset. For big plant setups allow Big Bud to reach approximately 50-60cm before inducing onset as an overall gain of approximately 60-85% can be expected, however if a surge of growth occurs above the given percentage, tying down will need to be implemented and in this case keep budding sites close.

This plant is very susceptible to mold so keep relative humidity below 65% to ensure finish, removing any dying leaves immediately. Halloween hairs on light green buds are captivating and finish comes at 56 days or 63 days with a conversation-stopping yield. Good resin coverage, particularly start of week nine with density and size of bud exceptional on either timeline. EC levels must be kept low and flush weekly ensuring a two-week flush to finish. Outdoor/greenhouse growers would need an arid climate or environmental control for success but what an example it would be with extended vegetation cycle. This is a very versatile variety, returning exceptional yields in any setup. After getting to know Big Bud with a couple of crops, most growers will see it established as 'Numero Uno!'

AROMA, TASTE AND EFFECT

When cut, the bud has an aroma of Juicy Fruit gum. It transitions to taste in a fruity, sweet flavor that leaves the palate with a cocktail of fruits like apples, pears and peaches. It has a very solid effect both in the head and body. With a heavy, sedative stone, it is excellent to wind down with at the end of the day or before bed or any recreational input. If required the effect is of a long duration, when buds have been dried over four weeks in the dark.

WATERING ⊞

Extensive root system ready for transplant.

WATERING

This is an area responsible for many growers' problems. Plants crave light and water but also oxygen, the more the merrier, as hydroponic growing proves. It is essential in soil that a plentiful supply of oxygen gets to the roots. If soil is kept in a wet state roots die off from no oxygen, resulting in a buildup of harmful odors and rotting from constant wetness.

CUTTINGS

Cuttings in rockwool only need to be watered every two to three days if no heat pad is used and if the room is not excessively warm. Allowing rockwool to become damp, as opposed to keeping wet, after second week encourages roots to form and search for moisture which is never far away.

Do not sit rockwool in water to offset having to water the cuttings as this encourages rot or slow root formation. If using a propagator tray use a second outer tray to fill with water or feed depending on what stage your cuttings are at. Lower the inner tray of cubes into the filled second outer tray, leave for five to 10 minutes and they are all done; replace the inner tray of cubes back into original outer tray with very little runoff. Do this every two to three days and roots will appear after eight to 12 days.

SOIL/COCO-COIR

After transferring cubes into pots of soil or coco-coir, use a root sensitizer to alleviate transplant shock and encourage extra root growth. In a 15cm pot approximately 150ml of water with a root sensitizer added should be poured around the stem area, slowly allowing the rest of the soil to absorb it but keeping the peripheral soil free from soaking and thus permitting oxygen to travel through the dry/damp perimeter, prefect conditions for vigorous root production at an early stage.

The soil should not be allowed to dry hard further than the surface; try to time most feeds just before surface dries, when it's patchy or still dark-looking—lift the pot and the heft or lightness will confirm one way or the other. Also look at the lowest set of leaves as these are the first to show the drooping signs familiar with low water.

As the new plants take hold increase watering by another 50-100ml depending on size and rate of consumption. Always err on the side of less, as plants always benefit from little and often, several smaller deliveries amounting to the original single delivery drives them crazy as soil remains a perfect consistency for oxygenation and dampness for roots to thrive in. If single deliveries are used (for personal growers, hand watering setups), ensure no more than a trickle of runoff, if any. A plant going into onset in a 25cm pot needs one liter maximum delivery to avoid soaking.

When plants are raging and if convenient, it is better when

hand watering to give a delivery as lights come on in a volume that will allow them to require another watering prior to lights out. Using the above example of one liter per 25cm pot, ideally the first delivery of 600ml would come when lights come on, then the second delivery of 400ml one to two hours prior to lights out (digital timers make easy work of staggered deliveries). This will leave the soil in a perfect condition through the dark period and ready for the morning, but always lift the pot if soil has not dried and leave alone if not light enough or surface looks and feels damp as opposed to patchy or dry.

As buds get into the seventh week, humidity will rise so try to avoid watering less than three hours prior to lights out. Regarding auto-feeding, a digital timer would be needed for soil due to extremely low delivery times, in some cases a matter of seconds. When system is set up and ready to run, first turn on the pump and time how long it takes from switching on to filling a marked jug to 75ml. Pot size is 25cm using coco-coir. If the plant is small and needs development then the above delivery volume may take eight seconds depending on setup. Two deliveries over 18 hours will equate to 150ml, so soil should remain damp, not wet or soaked. Simply adjust your deliveries based on the example given.

As plants grow, increase the number of deliveries slowly. Increments of one prevent gardeners getting carried away and overwatering. As water travels through damp/dry soil, it pulls behind it fresh air that vitalizes the roots, promoting perfect growing conditions. Again, oxygen is crucial: the more the better.

ROCKWOOL

New cuttings introduced into the main room do not require the regular feeding regimes of mature plants. Flood and drain cuttings in clay tray/pots need only three x 5-minute deliveries until maturity begins and extra deliveries are added, one at a time to coincide with growth requirements. Depending on setup but at peak requirements, a 5-minute delivery every two hours is the maximum through onset, shutting down through lights off cycle. NFT (Nutrient Film Technique) systems do not require 24-hour continuous running as roots are invariably protected from drying out by the system's canopy.

A 15-minute delivery every hour over 24 hours is sufficient in most NFT-type systems. Deliveries are affected if excessive roots are blocking an easy path for water to flow, or excessive heat is causing evaporation under the canopy, or deliveries are supplied by a small pump. In such cases continual running may be necessary. Cuttings freshly rooted for example would only require a two x 5-minute delivery over 24 hours, until they settle down, with extra deliveries being added as the plant progresses.

This is a loose guide, but again I emphasize that more is NOT better. Large rockwool cubes stay wet longer and cuttings (newly rooted) may only require one delivery per day. The message is OXYGEN. Plants adore mineral water straight from the bottle, carbon dioxide delivered directly to the roots. Generic brands are cheap and every now and then treat them. Do not PH adjust it or add anything to it; treat it as a flush.

This mother is hand-watered every day with 1 litre single delivery.

BLUEBERRY

FLOWER PERIOD: 63 days
APPROX. FINISHED ON-SET HEIGHT: 100-130%
MAXIMUM RELATIVE HUMIDITY: 85%

MAXIMUM TDS / EC: 1.4 / CF: 14 / PPM: 980
3 x 600 WATT x 25cm POT / YIELD = 85gms+

This variety is a specialty strain—the bud is in a league of its own for people into flavor and aromas; it's a gourmet's delight. This phenotype grows quickly although other phenotypes among the seeds which I was not lucky enough to score in this purchase describe a plant with mainly Indica traits. This one produces many widely staggered nodal points off the main stem; as laterals develop later in life they quickly move away from the center, opening the structure up and allowing light good access to budding sites. This model was tipped for research and this subsequently compromised the yield. As a large single stemmer, this variety has to be tied down, keeping budding sites close and maximizing yield potential. Laterals develop and grow quickly, promoting a proliferation of secondaries that form a fine lattice between the limbs. Flowering early at approximately 25cms is an option to develop a shorter plant; alternatively, for a large plant setup, allow Blueberry to reach 50-60cm before inducing onset, as a gain of approximately 100-130% can be expected and tying down is a growth surge necessity.

Multiple single stem setups would only need a short vegetation cycle after rooting, allowing cuttings to reach 15-20cm before inducing onset. Keep EC levels low and flush regularly and ensure a two-week flush to finish. This strain is very resilient to mold, tolerating relative humidity 80% and quite possibly higher. Always control your environment where possible even with mold-resistant strains as prevention is better than 'no' cure. The buds remain fluffy up to start of week seven, when hardening and resin production starts.

Greenhouse/outdoors is where this strain flourishes, getting strength from winds and the sun transmitting many other significant values vital to the plant's finish, along with every shade of blue imaginable. With extended vegetation cycle, this variety outdoors returns premium quality connoisseur smoke and in heavy yields. It does not have a strong aroma when growing unless disturbed. This product jars for long periods extremely well, becoming more blue the longer it is stored and cured. Blueberry grown outside and jarred over six months tastes like blueberry yoghurt and goes down likewise. The berry aroma from the jar has real body behind it. This is an exciting strain to have and I am looking forward to an Indica phenotype in my next purchase.

AROMA, TASTE AND EFFECT

When the bud is cut the indoor version has a strong blueberry aroma which erupts with an earthiness to it. This transitions to taste exceptionally well as you would hope, replicating the aroma. The inhale has the bold 'berry' flavor shinning through; the exhale holds the earthiness that reacts with the palate the same way a dry wine does; after a few seconds this fades away to leave the berry flavor to savour. Indoor Blueberry I found uplifting and motivational, excellent after breakfast and this euphoric feeling has a long duration. Outdoor Blueberry is very sedative to head and body, excellent for unwinding with at the end of the day or evenings in. Curing and storing alleviates the earthiness from indoor Blueberry and brings out much more fruit. The nugs turn bluer than blue over time resembling a science fiction bud.

CURED BUD

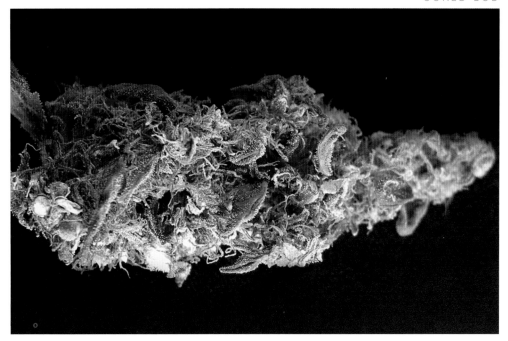

CURED BUD/CLOSEUP

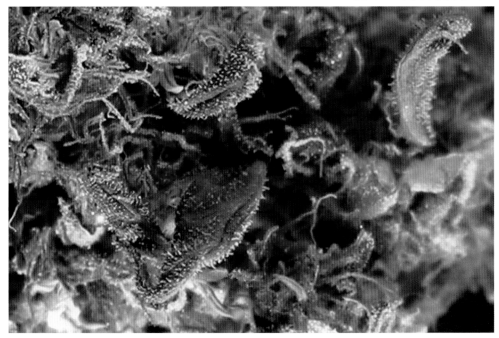

BLUE THUNDER

FLOWER PERIOD: 63 days
APPROX. FINISHED ON-SET HEIGHT: 100-120%
MAXIMUM RELATIVE HUMIDITY: 75-80%

MAXIMUM TDS / EC: 1.4 / CF: 14 / PPM: 980
3 x 600 WATT x 25cm POT / YIELD = 135gms+

Blue Thunder is a fast-paced grower, developing distanced, staggered nodal points that ensure fewer laterals will develop for an uncrowded, open format later in life or when tipped. Leaves are of medium size and dark green with a blue hue to them and low in number, along with a liberal scattering of fans allowing light good access to budding sites. Tipping will trigger a prolific surge in lateral growth with secondary development creating a maze between the laterals and giving the appearance of a tumbleweed of heads. (This model used is a single stem).

For a large indoor plant, tip at approximately 25-30cm ensuring a high number of laterals that move away from center with profuse secondary growth. For a shorter version, tip and induce onset at 25-30cm. Alternatively, take cuttings from a mother one week into onset to engage lateral growth immediately on striking, to develop a multi-limbed, open format right from the start. For multiple single stem setups, Blue Thunder only requires a little vegetation time after rooting; allow cutting to reach 15-20cm before inducing onset. Setups using large plants allow Blue Thunder to reach approximately 50-60cm, and inducing onset will result in a gain of approximately 100-120%. Whether a large single stem or tipped 'tumbleweed' structure, the growth surge through onset will cause budding sites to stretch before growth slows, therefore tying down either format will control height and keep budding sites close through this period. Buds remain soft and hairy till start of week six when resin production begins and buds start swelling.

Blue Thunder has a high resilience to mold, tolerating relative humidity of 75% and possibly a little higher. Very high calyx to leaf ratio, and dead or dying leaves are easy to spot and remove immediately. Keep EC levels low, flushing weekly, and ensure a two-week flush to finish. Outdoor/greenhouse growers should have excellent results capitalizing on the long vegetation cycle; using tying down, tipping or both should herald some excessive returns of connoisseur-grade herb.

AROMA, TASTE AND EFFECT

The aroma of the bud when cut is a combination of pineapple and lemon, extremely fruity and refreshing. The flavor, however, is full on ammonia, extremely acrid as is the burn-off which soon fills the room. This taste has to be acquired over two to three tokes for growers preferring fruity or floral flavors, but once acquired it quickly becomes an established favorite. The effect is sedative with a heavy delivery to the head, and the body has to relax. Excellent to unwind with or for evenings in, and the duration is extensive with little taper off.

CURED BUD

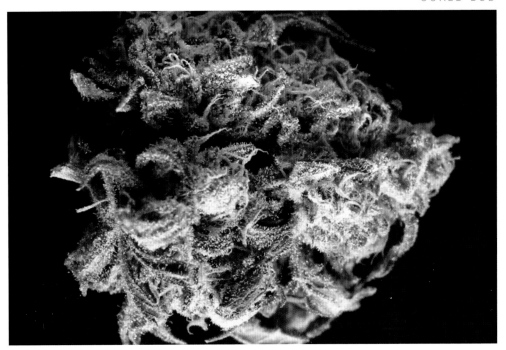

CURED BUD/CLOSEUP

BUBBLEBERRY

FLOWER PERIOD: 63-70 days
APPROX. FINISHED ON-SET HEIGHT: 100%-130%
MAXIMUM RELATIVE HUMIDITY: 80%

MAXIMUM TDS / EC: 1.4 / CF: 14 / PPM: 980
3 x 400 WATT x 25cm POT / YIELD = 80gms+

Bubbleberry is a personal favorite of mine, producing closely staggered nodal points that later in life, or if tipped, produce a high number of laterals that stay close to the center stem and create a tower format with a prolific development of secondaries. This is an excellent variety for close growing conditions as there is no spread. Leaves are minimal apart from those around budding sites and are mainly medium-sized, with rounded serration and a scattering of fans unless hydroed. In large plant setups, tip Bubbleberry at approximately 25-30cm to ensure a high number of laterals. A prolific development of secondaries fills in the gaps between laterals for very congested looking stems.

If height restrictions apply induce onset at approximately 25cm coinciding with a tipping to offset 12-hour response. For a large plant setup allow Bubbleberry to reach 50-60cm before inducing onset; tying down will be a necessity to offset growth surge. Hydroponic setups will see prolific growth through first four weeks of onset so inducing at 40cm may be more beneficial, with a vertical gain of approximately 100-130% to be expected. In multiple single stem setups Bubbleberry needs little vegetation time; allow cutting to reach 15-20cm before inducing onset. Excellent resistance to mold, tolerating 75% and possibly 80% humidity. I also had the opportunity to test this strain on spider mite, which used Bubbleberry as transport into the main setup without any identifying signs and completely dispersed onto neighboring plants!

Buds are slow to develop but incredibly close on all stems considering this plant's speed of growth, particularly through onset, making for extremely long colas that are finished 63 days. Home growers will want to go to 70 days just to ensure full finish. Bubbleberry will continue producing new white stigmas on top portions of buds and colas that are hard pushed to go brown even at 12 weeks. Keep EC levels low, flushing regularly, ensuring a two-week flush to finish. Resin and hardening begin at start of week six as colas remain Sativa-looking, with many leaves fading off beginning an unbelievable color spectrum. By 63 days resin is copious and ready with an incredible aroma if disturbed.

Outdoor/greenhouse growers will have excellent results with extended vegetation cycle and tipping plus tying down. That, coupled with its good mold and mite resistance, will quickly make Bubbleberry develop into a favorite. This strain is extremely versatile and suited to most setups, delivering gourmet buds of the highest distinction.

AROMA, TASTE AND EFFECT

This aroma is unquestionably unique, with a strong berry fragrance that has equal Bubblegum influence, placing this aroma on the candy (sweets, lollies) shelf. The taste is an intoxicating transition that does not require any palate experience whatsoever; every toker is speechless at the experience within seconds. A very solid cerebral high that expands as the minutes go by and encourages the body to relax. The duration is extensive and ideal to unwind with at the end of the day and on evenings spent in. This herb stores exceptionally well, turning more blue with age and, like Blueberry, resembling something from a science fiction movie.

CURED BUD

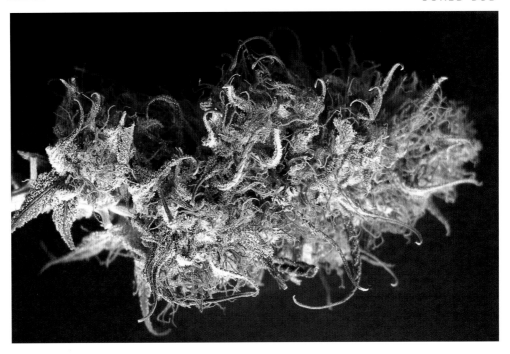

CURED BUD/CLOSEUP

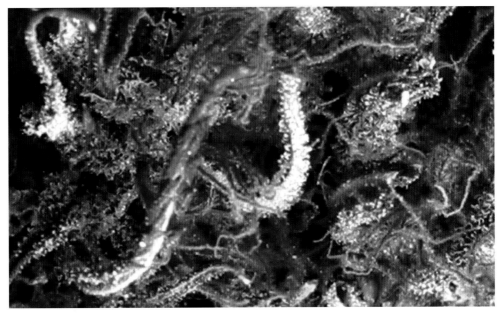

BUBBLEGUM #1

FLOWER PERIOD: 63 days
APPROX. FINISHED ON-SET HEIGHT: 100-130%+
MAXIMUM RELATIVE HUMIDITY: 70-75%

MAXIMUM TDS / EC: 1.4 / CF: 14 / PPM: 980
3 x 600 WATT x 25cm POT / YIELD = 150gms+

Another flavorful example from the industry, this variety is a rapid grower from the start. It has a Sativa appearance, with large 'ladyfinger' leaf structure, developing widely staggered nodal points off the main stem. These produce a format low in lateral numbers that move away from center, creating a vast spread with profuse secondary development that can form very large, dense buds if tied down. Excellent in a multiple single stem setup, in which cuttings require virtually no vegetation time after rooting; allow 3-7 days or approximately 15-20cm before inducing onset. In a large plant setup allow Bubblegum to reach at least 50-60cm (depending on finished size requirements) before inducing onset as a gain of approximately 100-130% can be expected.

Tipping and tying down work extremely well, allowing Bubblegum to fully develop and remain at low height. If height restrictions apply for personal setups, induce onset with a tipping at approximately 20-25cm. This strain has good resistance to mold, tolerating relative humidity 75%, good news for outdoor/greenhouse setups, although it is not impregnable. With an extended vegetation cycle this strain can easily become a tree with comparable yields. Tying down will be a necessity to maximize yield and keep plants out of sight.

Bubblegum is very durable and suited to any type of setup. The yield potential is excessive and consistent. Resin production and hardening begin at start of week seven. Keep EC levels low and flush frequently, ensuring a two-week flush to finish. Bubblegum's format of tightly grouped budding sites on all limbs pro-duces a tree of dense, sparkling colas with high calyx to leaf ratio and copious resin coverage and there is very little manicuring necessary after drying. This variety delivers excessive returns of a highly flavorful, potent herb with the effect of a mule kick by 63 days. Personal growers may want to harvest at 70 days, just to ensure the complete finish.

AROMA, TASTE AND EFFECT

This is gourmet bud: when cut after four weeks drying in the dark the aroma is sweet bubblegum with extremely pleasant undertones of holly, and transitions to taste exceptionally well. The palate is refreshed and after the exhale, left to savour a very familiar aftertaste. The effect is potent, with very heavy delivery to the head and body that encourages silence or napping, excellent for the end of the day, evenings in or weekends. The duration of the effect is long and increases before a very prolonged taper off. Any grower investing in this strain will be extremely satisfied.

CURED BUD

CURED BUD/CLOSEUP

LIGHTING & TEMPERATURE ⊞

For the personal grower the requirement for variety brings its own headache as variety translates into staggered growth patterns, vegetation cycles, and flowering cycles, and differing resistance to humidity. One aim of this book is to aid growers in achieving multiple strains within the same crop.

Some growers use a three-day continuous dark period to finish. This does send most varieties into a resin frenzy, but humidity must be controlled as this is when it's highest and three days dark for me is a bit scary!

Be careful of excessive cold even during lights on. Cold temperatures tell the plants the environment could produce frost, a deadly enemy for many species of plants. Resin is not required in this situation and although production doesn't cease altogether it is very minimal. Instead the plant produces a robust growth of leaves of all sizes and it becomes almost like a lettuce, with very little development of buds. Temperatures around 8°C-14°C through the lights-off period will require additional heating if the grower is to avoid this adverse effect. Temperatures during lights off need to be at least 18°C to encourage standard development. During lights on, be careful of temperatures not exceeding 30°C as buds will open and become fingers as opposed to the tight, dense look. This is natural as it aids with air flow to offset mold in such conditions.

Removal of healthy leaves in order to allow light down to secondary branches is a debatable point; this action can unnecessarily stress the plant and affect the cycle it is undergoing. However, it is by far better to cut the offending leaf blade across the width of the leaf, thereby removing 50% of it and hopefully exposing the area in question without shocking the plant.

When using lights it is important to know penetration depths of the bulbs being used. A 400-watt light has approximately a 12" penetration ability, after that the lumens decrease. A 600-watt has approximately 18" penetration capacity. Heat shields can be attached to most makes of lamps and they provide excellent light dispersal, first removing the heat directly beneath the bulb and allowing plant tops closer proximity to the penetration field. Second, the light is reflected off the surface of the shield back up to the shade, which reflects the light down evenly over the entire area of the shade and eliminates the bright spot, and plants wherever positioned grow vertically and do not lean in toward the bulb, obstructing light.

Finished results of a "too cold" environment

✛ HYDRO HINTS

Hydroponic growth, particularly during 18 hour cycle can be phenomenal, certainly an area that hydroponic cuts down on time. I found the leaf size to be considerably large, along with stem girth. It is quite difficult to slow growth using conventional methods as they recover so quickly. They are capable of producing large crops with relative ease. However, if you get a problem i.e. pythium, it will infest the whole crop in the next automatic feed and it would have to be addressed immediately it is identified.

Growers using hydro set-ups can also fall prey to overwatering causing root rot and an awful aroma from stagnation. Here are some general figures for most hydro set-ups: newly rooted cuttings require 3 x 4 minute feeds over 18 hours i.e. lights-on, midway and last delivery an hour before lights-off. No delivery till lights come on again. As plant responds add a extra delivery allowing time for plant to respond before adding another. Maximum delivery usually begins from on-set with a maximum of 6 x 5 minute deliveries over 12 hour lights-on cycle. 2 weeks prior to finish, deliveries should begin reducing 1 delivery a week to finish on 4. This would vary according to many factors but the principle remains – more is not better!

Most mediums will remain moist to wet below the surface for some hours, allowing volumes of oxygen to the roots essential for a healthy, big plant they only need one feed during lights-off period (budding plants) but should start the feed cycle to coincide with the lights coming on.

Hydroponic plants tend to remain green throughout their budding cycle which has an attraction of its own. None the less, different they may be but impressive they certainly are. PH is taken in the reservoir daily and adjusted if needed, and usually does, along with TDS readings.

Never add just nutrient to the reservoir without the correct dilution of fresh water (topping-up) as water evaporates leaving salts behind (white markings) that build up and

The Notorious London Cabbie with a treasured AK47 (1 plant shown) grown in hydro Dutch Pot System. Photo credit: NLC

elevate the PH levels. Flushing is vital as the reserve of salts they store during standard feeding is high and must be forced to deplete so as not to effect the herb as a finished product.

Flushing with water over a 2 week period (remembering to only use the minimum amount of water in the reservoir as each day it has to be emptied as the nutrient in the systems media, will continue to contaminate the water on its return to the reservoir. Using a small volume of water is just easy work and by placing a weighted container, i.e. 5 litre bucket into reservoir will raise the low water level.

Water in the reservoir requires good continuous aeration, invest in a decent pump. Checks need to be kept on the rockwool itself particularly in hot conditions as water evaporates leaving the salts behind and in slabs the PH can be extreme, flush using watering can if reservoir change is a drama and run an extension of hose or piping from the outlet to a bucket but not back into the reservoir.

BUBBLEGUM #2

FLOWER PERIOD: 56-63 days
APPROX. FINISHED ON-SET HEIGHT: 50-80%
MAXIMUM RELATIVE HUMIDITY: 70%

MAXIMUM TDS / EC: 1.4 / CF: 14 / PPM: 980
3 x 600 WATT x 25cm POT / YIELD = 130gms+

This is a slow-paced grower, producing closely staggered nodal points that ensure a proliferation of lateral growth later in life or if tipped. Large plant setups should allow Bubblegum to reach approximately 25-30cm before tipping to ensure that a high number of laterals develop slowing moving away from center, with staggered secondaries. Leaves are large with round serration and typical of Indica, and fade and color toward the finish. Some large leaves do impede light, and for personal growers it will be beneficial to remove 50% of each leaf in certain areas of the plant to allow light into budding sites.

In large plant setups, allow Bubblegum to reach approximately 50-60cm before inducing onset, as an overall gain of 50-70% can be expected. In multiple single stem setups extra vegetation time will be necessary; allow cuttings to reach 20-25cm before inducing onset. Keep EC levels low and flush weekly, ensuring a two-week flush to finish for optimum results.

This strain has good resistance to mold, tolerating relative humidity of 70% and possibly higher. Outdoor/greenhouse growers will be very pleased with this purchase, and particularly with an extended vegetation period it should develop into a short, compact treetop. Depending on size, tying down will facilitate in keeping development of budding sites close, and allow the plant to reach full potential while keeping out of sight. Watch for unexpected prolonged wet climate nearing finish, and harvest early, such is the size and density of Bubblegum's fruit. Mild climates should see success, but that likelihood will have been determined by the grower by scrutinizing the strain's individual characteristics before purchase. The finished product is alive with resin and secondaries resembling golf balls. This is a very high quality product delivering a connoisseur gourmet smoke.

AROMA, TASTE AND EFFECT

The aroma from a disturbed flowering bud will make you want to pop it into your mouth and begin bubble-blowing, it is that convincing. After drying, this fragrance is slightly diminished but still retains the bubblegum comparison. The resin content is thick and when bud is chopped up it appears as a melt in the bowl. The taste is shockingly delightful—acrid, distinctly ammonia-like, real sharp—and is carried in the burn off and permeates the room quickly. For tokers preferring fruity or floral flavors, this variety will require two or three hits to acquire the taste, but once discovered it is hard to beat. The effect is an immediate, heavy cerebral delivery; but this is not a deep, removed state of mind, rather euphoric and uplifting. The body is left undisturbed, making this excellent after breakfast with coffee. The effect has a long duration with an impressively prolonged taper off.

CURED BUD

CURED BUD/CLOSEUP

CARAMELLA

FLOWER PERIOD: 56 days
APPROX. FINISHED ON-SET HEIGHT: 50-80%
MAXIMUM RELATIVE HUMIDITY: 65%

MAXIMUM TDS / EC: 1.4 / CF: 14 / PPM: 980
3 x 600 WATT x 25cm POT / YIELD = 130gms+

This strain is a slow grower, producing many staggered nodal points off the main stem, which guarantees a profuse development of laterals if the plant is allowed to fully mature or tipping is used. Leaves are of a medium/large format on overly long stems allowing maximum light to pass unhindered, and they remain a dark green throughout. In big plant setups, allow Caramella to reach approximately 25-30cm before tipping, to ensure a high number of laterals that slowly move away from center, opening the structure up with a profuse development of secondaries and giving the limbs a very congested appearance. Ensure a good size is achieved in large plant setups, approximately 50-60cm, prior to onset and expect an overall gain of approximately 50-80%.

This strain does not like a humid environment whatsoever so ensure from onset that relative humidity is below 65%, and after week 6 to below 60% for peace of mind, if possible. The buds/colas are slow to develop, getting into gear start of week six with hardening and resin production. By 56 days they resemble concrete, extremely dense and ready. In multiple single stem set ups, allow extra vegetation time and inducing on set at approximately 20-25cm for some very impressive stems of high calyx to leaf buds.

Outdoor/greenhouse will have exceptional results but beware of Caramella's disposition to humidity. Environmental control or arid climate is a necessity to finish this strain, but with the extended vegetation period and tying down, it will return excessive yields. Keep EC levels low and flush once per week, ensuring a two-week flush to finish for optimal results. Very few leaves are left at the finish making manicuring after a four-week dry in the dark very quick.

AROMA, TASTE AND EFFECT

When Caramella is growing, there is a sweet honeyed aroma to the buds. When dried and cut, this disappears and is replaced by a sharp aroma of pineapple. The taste is different again, resembling figs and dates with hashy undertones, very pleasant indeed. The effect is very cerebral; it rocks the head for a short while and then focus comes. The body is fairly unaffected unless this strain is overindulged in. The duration is long making this an excellent herb for people on the move, and for creativity and concentrating. It's ideal after breakfast with coffee. Caramella is also ideal at the end of the day or evenings as 'servings' through this period tend to be more copious and this moves Caramella into a more sedative effect. This is a genuine 'all-rounder' from growth to indulgence factors.

CURED BUD

CURED BUD/CLOSEUP

CHRONIC

FLOWER PERIOD: 56-63 days
APPROX. FINISHED ON-SET HEIGHT: 50-75%
MAXIMUM RELATIVE HUMIDITY: 65%

MAXIMUM TDS / EC: 1.4 / CF: 14 / PPM: 980
3 x 600 WATT x 25cm POT / YIELD = 140gms+

This is a slow-paced grower for a 50/50 cross, producing closely staggered nodal points off the main stem, with medium to large leaves that remain light green throughout life cycle. Tipping will compromise Chronic's yield; this plant has such profuse development of laterals and secondaries after maturity, aided by its slow-paced growth, that tipping should be avoided. Instead take cuttings from a mother one week into onset as this will engage lateral growth immediately after rooting, developing a multi-limbed open format from the start and retaining the center stem. For setups requiring excessive returns using fewer plants, Chronic is hard to beat. The prolific growth of secondaries off the laterals reflects Chronic's yield potential; the plant consistently sports a forearm/calf-sized center column. Multiple single stem setups would require extra vegetation time, inducing onset at approximately 20-25cm.

Low EC rates with regular flushing work particularly well ensuring a two-week flush to finish for the best results. For big indoor plants, ensure a good size is reached, 50-60cm, before inducing onset as an overall gain of approximately 50-75% can be expected. This variety cannot tolerate high humidity and has to be kept below 65% till start of week 6, then reduce further if possible, to below 60% for the finish. The buds remain hairy to week six when they begin to harden and resin production really picks up. Chronic may be harvested at 56 days, producing an excessive-sized center cola, personal growers will want to harvest 63 days to ensure the complete finish and produce a noticeable increase in yield, resin coverage, and effect.

Outdoor/greenhouse growers will require environmental control or arid conditions to ensure the finish. As a big plant with extended vegetation period, Chronic will return excessive yields. A high calyx to leaf ratio means manicuring is quick after drying. This variety produces solid weight all over, not just the main colas, and this highlights the need for good light all over the plant through all cycles, and maximum reflection indoors. Chronic is an extremely versatile strain responding excessively in most setups and could be described as a 'Super Heavy-Weight.'

AROMA, TASTE AND EFFECT

The aroma is floral when cut; light and delicate, resembling wildflowers. There is sweetness to the aroma yet none of this transitions to taste; instead the taste reflects dates and figs with hashy undertones leaving the palate with sundry rich exotic flavors to savour. The effect is cerebrally uplifting and energetic, leaving the body unaffected. This encourages social activities or physical engagement so it's perfect for people on the move. This strain is ideal after breakfast with coffee. It has an effect of long duration if required. Larger doses of Chronic, i.e., bongs, will sedate—for example, one cone wasted me!

CURED BUD

CURED BUD/CLOSEUP

CINDERELLA 99 F2

FLOWER PERIOD: 56-63 days
APPROX. FINISHED ON-SET HEIGHT: 50-70%
MAXIMUM RELATIVE HUMIDITY: 75%

MAXIMUM TDS / EC: 1.4 / CF: 14 / PPM: 980
3 x 600 WATT x 25cm POT / YIELD = 140gms+

This strain reflects all the traits of a Sativa except growth, which in this case is slow. This works to a great advantage in achieving a short plant otherwise reflecting all the Sativa traits. Cinderella produces closely staggered nodal points ensuring a proliferation of lateral growth later in life or if tipped. Large plant setups should allow Cinderella to reach 25-30cm before tipping to ensure a high number of laterals, which slowly move away from center with plenty of secondary development and a very congested format. Leaves are medium sized with a Sativa appearance and a liberal scattering of 'ladyfinger' fans.

This strain has good mold resistance, tolerating relative humidity of 75%. For an indoor big plant, allow Cinderella to reach 50-60cm before inducing onset as an overall gain of approximately 50-70% can be expected. In a multiple single stem setup Cinderella will require extra vegetation time; allow cutting to reach 20-25cm before inducing onset. Resin and hardening begins at the start of week six and Cinderella is very impressive at 56 days with rock-hard, Sativa-shaped colas and an excellent coating of resin. Both these factors increase noticeably if allowed to run to 63 days. Keep EC levels low and flush weekly, ensuring a two-week flush to finish.

Outdoor/greenhouse growers will have excellent results with extended vegetation period, and coupled with its good mold resistance, this would be an extremely rewarding and enjoyable purchase. The buds and colas pack the stems, helped by the very slow growth; the budding sites lock up the stem from the dirt up (good reflection helps) dense and resin adorned, there's no trim whatsoever, and the high calyx to leaf ratio means virtually no manicuring after drying. This is a milestone for me in growing a Sativa plant with an Indica growth pattern.

AROMA, TASTE AND EFFECT

The aroma of the bud while growing is citrus/grapefruit with real body, it literally erupts when disturbed. After four weeks of drying in the dark, the bud's aroma changes from citrus to musky grapefruit. This transitions to taste extremely well: novices educating their palates will enjoy using this example. The musky grapefruit taste is extremely long lasting as is the effect, a strong Sativa-style delivery to the head washing away immediate thoughts while quickly reaching the body. This herb expands the mind and is excellent for creativity, otherwise best indulged in at the end of the day or on evenings in, as the duration of the effect is exceptionally long with little taper off and no ceiling level. This herb's aroma and taste are truly gourmet and really sets this plant apart form all others—a superb product.

CURED BUD

CURED BUD/CLOSEUP

CUTTINGS +

Cuttings are the most important step in becoming an independent grower. Many associated products on the shelf work for some yet others can't seem to come to grips with. Wax gives good results and is very reliable. Wetting agents can be used prior to the wax treatment to facilitate the wax's adherence to the plant's surface.

Prepare the work area ensuring segregated areas of a bench for each step, using clean utensils and a slender glass to pour the wax into.

Soak rockwool propagator cubes in treated water or dehumidifier/air-conditioning run-off or bottled water with a root stimulator.

Try to take them as low down the main stem as permitted. Unless a mother plant is being used for quantity, a cutting of approximately 10-15cm+ is adequate.

Take a glass of fizzy mineral water to place cuttings into when removed from the mother. Carbonated mineral water really gives them a lift and counteracts the shock they suffer.

Now the cutting is ready for the final cut to the stem. Remove from glass, choose an area at least 3/4" from the original cut, and with the scissors gently scrape a 1/2" area until the rough surface is replaced by a silky smooth moist surface, rotating the stem so as to treat the full circumference of area.

In the center of the prepared surface cut at an angle.

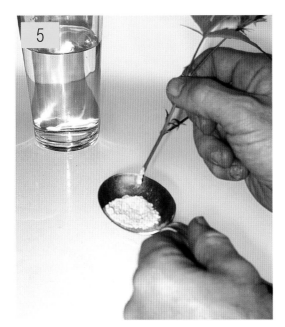

Place back into mineral water if using powder (if using gel dip as soon as cut), then roll end through the rooting powder.

Leave up to three or four leaves, cutting in half across the blades to improve transpiration.

Holding the stem, dip cutting into container of wax ensuring full coverage of leaves.

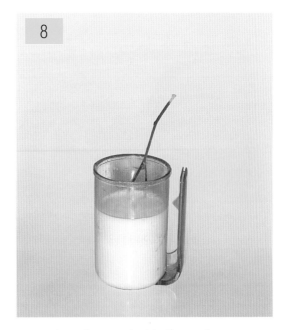

Leave for approximately 10 seconds.

Allow excess to run off back into the container.

Now place cutting into cube.

Place each cutting into the propagator tray. No hood is required as the wax provides a personal hood for each cutting. No heat pad required either, just a warm environment provided by a 24 hour light cycle for the first week which really helps their transition and offsets shock.

Wax can be poured back into its container and reused until an obvious long period has passed or you run out.

Do not allow cubes to dry out but do not leave water on floor of propagator. When blocks need moistening, make a solution using bottled spring water or water from the dehumidifier and root sensitiser for the first week after which add a hydroponic nutrient A + B at a ratio of 1ml A and 1ml B to 1 litre water plus a root stimulator.

Apply the feeds by using a second propagator outer tray pour the mix to fill tray approximately halfway, remove the inner tray the cuttings sit on and lower into nutrient filled tray, nutrient should come 1/3 -1/2 the height of the cubes, leave for 10 minutes. Lift inner tray out and place back into original outer tray and place back under fluorescents. Cubes should be fine for 2-3 days before next soak, just monitor them. No foliar feeding what so ever and roots should come through after 8-12 days, environment pending.

Ten-day-old waxed cuttings.

EL NIÑO

FLOWER PERIOD: 56-63 days
APPROX. FINISHED ON-SET HEIGHT: 100-130%
MAXIMUM RELATIVE HUMIDITY: 65%

MAXIMUM TDS / EC: 1.4 / CF: 14 / PPM: 980
3 x 400 WATT x 25cm POT / YIELD = 85gms+

This is an established strain offering the grower excellent yields of premium grade herb. It's a fast-paced grower after rooting, producing distanced staggered nodal points that produce fewer laterals that, when mature, do not stray far from center giving a tower format and making the plant excellent for close quarter growing. Secondary development is prolific giving the limbs a very busy, congested appearance. Leaves are medium with a liberal scattering of broad, round, serrated fans that are lime-green throughout the life cycle. Tipping El Niño at approximately 25-30cm for large plant setups, ensures a high number of laterals.

Inducing onset on a plant at 50-60cm will result in a vertical gain of approximately 100-130%. Tying down will be necessary on big plants to offset height and maximize yield potential. Budding sites are very closely grouped from the dirt up and remain in this format through inducement of onset. As growth slows, budding sites lock up to build excessive, long colas. In multiple single stem setups El Niño would require little vegetation time after rooting, allowing cutting to reach 15-20cm before inducing onset.

Keep EC levels low, flushing weekly and ensuring a two-week flush to finish for optimum results. With its low toleration of mold, this strain requires a relative humidity below 65% for success. Outdoor/greenhouse setups require a fairly arid climate or environmental control to succeed, but coupled with extended vegetation cycle and tying down as a single stem or tipped, El Niño will return excessive yields. The buds respond to onset quickly and by start of week five resin production is fierce along with hardening; even the nugs just above the dirt are laden with resin and dense (if good reflection is used). No trim here; plants are finished at 56 days although personal growers will want to go to 63 days for a noticeable increase in yield and resin content and the complete finish. I always have a copy among my personals.

AROMA, TASTE AND EFFECT

The aroma from a cut bud is distinctly lemon curd (sandwich spread) with skunky overtones. Disturbing this plant through flowering can incite munchies. The aroma transitions to taste superbly well, saturating the palate with a lemon zest that will captivate you. The exhale has a stronger presence of skunk but still in the background, leaving a wonderful prolonged aftertaste. The effect is soothingly cerebral, promoting creative thinking; a touch too much and the effect is sedative. This bud is excellent to unwind with or after breakfast with coffee at weekends.

CURED BUD

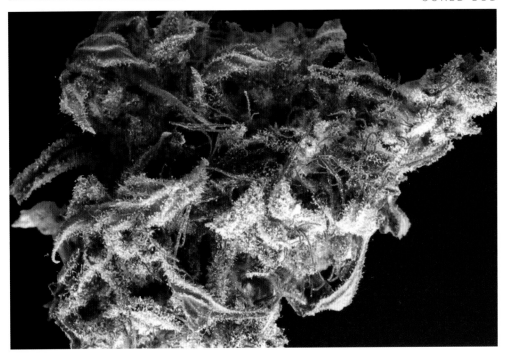

CURED BUD/CLOSEUP

G13

FLOWER PERIOD: 49-56 days
APPROX. FINISHED ON-SET HEIGHT: 50-75%
MAXIMUM RELATIVE HUMIDITY: 75%

MAXIMUM TDS / EC: 1.4 / CF: 14 / PPM: 980
3 x 400 WATT x 25cm POT / YIELD = 140gms+
MAXIMUM RESIN PRODUCTION AT 49 DAYS

This strain is supposedly affiliated to a US government research project and now available on the market. This is a very impressive variety, a slow-paced grower producing closely staggered nodal points that ensure a proliferation of laterals later in life or when tipped. Apart from the small leaves surrounding budding sites which literally 'cake up' with resin, G13 produces a few medium-sized, round-serrated, dark green leaves and a scattering of fans giving budding sites good access to light.

Tipping at 25-30cm, for a large plant setup, allows for the development of a high number of laterals that mature and slowly move away from center opening up G13's format. Very few secondaries develop off the multitude of laterals and this facilitates the crowded budding sites in developing to their maximum. In big plant setups, allow G13 to reach approximately 50-60cm before inducing onset as an overall gain of approximately 50-75% can be expected.

Multiple single stem setups will require extra vegetation time after rooting, allowing cutting to reach 20-25cm before inducing onset. This plant responds very quickly to onset and by start of week five the buds are hardening and resin production is fierce. It has excellent resistance to mold, tolerating relative humidity of 75% and possibly a little higher, although if environmental control is not possible, observe for dying leaves and remove immediately. Keep EC levels low, flushing weekly and ensuring a two-week flush to finish.

Outdoor/greenhouse setups should produce exceptional results allowing for the extended vegetation, high mold resistance, and short flower cycle that should stay ahead of seasonal change and aid with drying. G13's buds at 49 days are well pumped with a resin coverage that is one of the industry's best at that stage, with oversized colas that amazingly increase noticeably by 56 days and can exceed the size of forearms, with nugs (using good reflection) that 'drip' resin. From the dirt up buds are very dense and there is no trim on this plant; with its very high calyx to leaf ratio there is virtually no manicuring after drying four weeks in the dark. This is a very impressive product indeed that ranks in the upper echelons of the industry's varieties.

AROMA, TASTE AND EFFECT

A powerful sweet aniseed aroma erupts from a cut bud of G13. The taste is rich, blending dates and plums with hashy undertones. The exhale leaves a long aftertaste to savour. The effect is considered medicinal and extremely potent, delivering a mule kick to the head and a rugby tackle to the body, with a very prolonged effect that increases before unnoticeably tapering off. Only indulge during 'free time' and do not take lightly. Coning will induce a cough due to the incredible resin production.

Photo courtesy Smuttley

CURED BUD

CURED BUD/CLOSEUP

GREAT WHITE SHARK

FLOWER PERIOD: 56-63 days
APPROX. FINISHED ON-SET HEIGHT: 50-70%
MAXIMUM RELATIVE HUMIDITY: 65%

MAXIMUM TDS / EC: 1.4 / CF: 14 / PPM: 980
3 x 400 WATT x 25cm POT / YIELD = 90gms+

Shark is a slow-paced grower reflecting typical Indica traits. It develops closely staggered nodal points, ensuring a prolific development of lateral growth later in life or if tipped, opening Great White Shark up with new laterals slowly moving away from the main stem and with vigorous secondary development giving a big mature Shark a very busy, congested appearance. For large plant setups, tipping Great White Shark at 25-30cm will ensure that a greater number of laterals develop. Some leaves will require that 50% of the blade be removed to allow light to budding sites. The broad, round-serrated leaves remain a lime-green throughout vegetation and flowering stages.

For large indoor plants allow 50-60cm+ before inducing onset with an expected overall gain of approximately 50-70%. In multiple single stem setups Great White Shark will require extra vegetation time, allowing cuttings to reach approximately 20-25cm before inducing onset. This variety hates humidity so keep relative humidity below 65% to ensure the finish.

A very high calyx to leaf ratio guarantees quick manicuring and what small leaves there are receive thick resin coverage and stigmas turn bright orange by start of week five. Great White Shark has a very finished look at 49 days, with swollen buds and an abundance of resin. Both these factors will increase significantly over the last two weeks until the finished example is as humbling an experience to confront as the fish itself. Keep EC levels low and flush weekly, ensuring a two-week flush to finish for best results. Outdoor/greenhouse setups will need an arid climate or environmental control to succeed with Great White Shark, but with the extended vegetation cycle and slow growth, it should resemble a truncated tree!

AROMA, TASTE AND EFFECT

Great White Shark is another great product; the aroma of its chunky nugs is very fruity, a powerful cocktail of apples, pears and peaches. The taste is the aroma, unmistakably fruity and friendly. The inhale is sweet but the exhale loses this to some degree, leaving the palate to savour a mélange of fruity delights. It's a real pleasure to prepare for smoking. The smoke almost fizzes in the mouth—a sign for me of good potency! The effect is head and body on a sedative level. Excellent at the end of the day, or for evenings spent in, or on the weekend. The duration is extensive with no ceiling level. This is a high quality herb indeed, and dried over four weeks in the dark, Great White Shark will be at its best.

HAWAII X MALAWI

FLOWER PERIOD: 70 days
APPROX. FINISHED ON-SET HEIGHT: 100-130%
MAXIMUM RELATIVE HUMIDITY: 80%

MAXIMUM TDS / EC: 1.4 / CF: 14 / PPM: 980
3 x 400 WATT x 25cm POT / YIELD = 85gms+

This is preferably an outdoor strain, but it reacts well indoors as well and growers can be treated to a very unique flavored herb indeed with a high that expands the mind. Hawaii x Malawi is a fast-paced grower from rooting, producing widely staggered nodal points that produce fewer laterals to move away from center later in life or if tipped, to develop an open structure allowing good light access to all budding sites. In big plant setups, tip at approximately 25-30cm to ensure a high number of laterals. Leaves are medium-sized with a rounded serration and a few more in number than standard indoor varieties, with a liberal scattering of fans, many of which die off due to length of flower cycle.

In a multiple single stem setup, this cross would require little vegetation time after rooting, inducing onset at approximately 15-20cm . Alternatively for large plant setups, tying down this variety drastically improves yield and keeps budding sites close through onset surge. If height restrictions apply induce onset at approximately 25-30cm with a tipping to offset growth surge. A mature plant of 50-60cm when onset induced will gain approximately 100-130%. Budding sites become staggered with the growth surge forming a cluster toward the crown as the pace slows; the staggered formation aids with airflow as the buds can become impressively dense golf balls.

Keep EC levels low, flushing regularly and ensuring a two-week flush to finish. Outdoor/greenhouse growers will excel with this variety. With the long vegetation cycle it will require tying down for a substantial yield. It has a high resistance to mold, tolerating relative humidity up to 80%. Buds remain hairy till 49 days and over the next three weeks the daily transformation of hardening and resin production is hypnotic.

AROMA, TASTE AND EFFECT

The fragrance here is very individual—a strong lemon aroma accompanied by an underlying vanilla essence; when combined the aroma is lemon meringue, and this is very complex as fragrances go. The taste transitions exceptionally well, full-on lemon meringue pie with every toke. This is one of, if not currently THE most gourmet tastes I have smoked, like the clotted cream for a scone and jam. The palate will be as satisfied after each toke as with the dessert itself. The effect is sedative, making it perfect at the end of the day. The effect has an impressive duration if required, so if long breaks between tokes are happening then this is a good smoke. There is no ceiling level with the effect increasing before an unnoticeable taper off. Although I use through flower cycle an organic mix of nutrients, I can only wonder about and hope one day to sample an outdoor/greenhouse version of this strain!

HUMIDITY ⊞

Two types of dehumidifiers.

A topic that everyone wants to know about, but doesn't want. Well, there are ways to grow and flower for budget or small setups in high humidity when lights are off if a dehumidifier or air conditioner is not possible, and here are some notes that will help. The following information is primarily for home growers with a moderate to small garden and a limited budget requiring options other than air conditioners or dehumidifiers— the latter being the cheapest means of removing humidity regarding unit and running costs. However, a carbon filter/ozone extractor is essential, if fairly costly; remember what its function is.

Gardens utilizing a room in the house can have the grow room door open, using a number of ways to prevent light spilling out and allowing vast amounts of fresh air in. The extraction fan draws air from the room, which in turn pulls fresh air from the open door without too much reentering the house; adjusting the door position to reduce the opening will offset escaping air.

A 48cm fan at the door, pointing into the grow room, will ensure volumes of air are constantly being pushed in, helping to reduce temperatures. Also use a 48cm pedestal fan to move air between the tops of light reflectors and the ceiling of the grow room because over the lights-on cycle, heat rises and needs to be moved around. This is especially true before the need of the extraction filter, which does not necessarily have to be used until start of week four unless the 'green' aroma through vegetation cycle becomes too overpowering.

The size and volume of plants will determine humidity levels along with the climate. The extractor fan should be on continuously from start of fourth week when lights are on, as there is usually no scented aroma to this point, although there is after maturity a green vegetation aroma.

Utilize the extractor fan at night on a cycle of 15 minutes every 60-90 minutes in the case of no inlet, i.e., if a prepared window is used for extraction it may be the only window in the room and again certain circumstances may govern the use of outlet and inlet from one window. Enough air will return into the room naturally a minute or two after the 15 minute cycle (as door will be shut through lights-out period).

You should have one or two 48cm oscillating fans in the room during lights out moving air around constantly, and keep the watering cycle to when the lights come on so at lights-out the soil surface should be patchy or dry. Spacing between the plants, clearing lower section of stems free of insignificant secondary buildup, allows good airflow around the base of plants.

Choice of plant is important in conditions of high humidity. No buckets or reservoirs should be left exposed in grow room during lights-off period; cover with a lid to help improve the relative humidity.

Commercial moisture rids help particularly in the last three weeks of flowering. Using three to four of these will help as long as many other ideas are implemented. Six-hundred-watt lights are more conducive to producing the desired type of bud density that is otherwise severely affected by anything other than perfect conditions. Six-hundred-watt will be problematic, a four-hundred-watt setup would be more efficient under these circumstances, building good size without the really heavy density and associated increased possibility of mold. When lights switch off air must be exhausted immediately along with oscillation in the grow room to remove the hot/warm air and replace with fresh air.

Centrifugal fans used with carbon filters are ideal for quick extraction. When ducted up and set on a noise/vibration dampener the fans run fairly quietly, in fact it's the noise of air movement and the sound frequency that cuts down on its noise range capacity to travel, especially through brick and such materials. When coupled with a carbon filter this provides the best air extraction method available. WARNING: Centrifugal fans are extremely powerful. Check flow rates with handling capacity of filter. Standard speed is often too fast for the air to be cleaned thoroughly and odors will be released. A variable speed controller or light switch dimmer can be wired into the fan (by an electrical tradesman) and in most cases the fan's speed has to be retarded some 50%-75% to be efficient with the filter; some fans come with a built-in retarder. Regarding the need for an imbalance of air pressure in the grow room, achieved by slightly more air being exhausted (filtered out of the grow room) than air being pushed into the grow room via a second fan (which keeps fresh air circulating in the grow room): this can be achieved by using two different sized fans, the bigger of the two (seek advice for appropriate fan sizes for your setup) being used to remove air from the room. The smaller sized fan (one size down from the larger model will be perfect) is used to push fresh air into the grow room. This slight imbalance of air pressure will prevent air escaping from the grow room untreated. To test that the method is working, switch on both fans, light an incense or two and hold them where there are obvious openings to the grow room, i.e., around the door entrance or any joins that are not sealed. The incense smoke should be sucked into the gaps and through to the grow room, indicating the pressure is correct, and no air is escaping. This imbalance must not be too extreme as too much air removed from the room will encourage the temperature to rise. This solution cannot be approached 'half-cocked' (growers utilizing whatever is available, which invariably isn't suitable). Purchase the correct size fans with advice for a stealth system. Also, if it's possible, try to place the ballasts of the lighting equipment somewhere external to the grow room. Each box raises the temperature in a grow room by 1°c. Keep them raised off the floor for better air circulation on a metal-framed stand or equivalent, but do not stand ballast on timber as the constant heat it emits during on mode slowly dries the timber out, and by the third or fourth crop the timber can be like tinder, ready to ignite.

Be careful in optimizing the distance of the bulb from the plant tops for maximum lumens to travel down into the crop (approximately 12" penetration depth for a 400-watt) as although the leaves show no signs of heat stress, upward curling or fade, the colas absorb the heat surrounding them and actually warm up; subsequently when the lights go off, air cools but the center of the cola remains warm for some hours creating moisture as it cools in the colder environment. Night after night as the colas increase, more water is absorbed and stored which can lead to the inevitable, so place plants carefully around the shade, avoiding hot spots, and sacrifice a couple of extra inches above plant tops or use a heat shield. Also, reducing the volume or number of deliveries prevents the colas and buds from excessive building; as much as super-dense buds are the desired finish, they are easy prey to high humidity where it is not controlled.

These suggestions are for the budget grower and as extreme as these measures appear, dedication prevails. Dehumidifiers work excellently in relation to purchase price, running cost, and effectiveness. A small unit, approximately 220 watts, will reduce relative humidity by approximately 30% during the lights-off mode. This can be the difference between success and failure. It really gives peace of mind and two units work very impressively and will keep most rooms at a safe relative humidity.

Alternately, one portable air-conditioning unit will do the best job; it can run a high wattage, as well as being multi-purposed: it keeps room cool, controlling heat and insect proliferation, buds become more compact as opposed to opening out in hot temperatures, and collects and cleans plenty of run-off which can be poured into reservoir as recycling.

Carbon filter attached to a centrifugal fan.

HAZE 19 X SKUNK #1

FLOWER PERIOD: 56-63 days
APPROX. FINISHED ON-SET HEIGHT: 80-110%
MAXIMUM RELATIVE HUMIDITY: 65%

MAXIMUM TDS / EC: 1.4 / CF: 14 / PPM: 980
3 x 400 WATT x 25cm POT / YIELD = 125gms+

This was my first authentic Dutch grow after my second visit in 1992; the first visit was a bender! I had great results from this strain even at a novice level. Growing at a moderate rate throughout the vegetation cycle, it produces closely staggered nodal points (for a Haze cross) that reveal this strain's compact lateral structure (note this when selecting correct phenotype). In large plant setup, tip at approximately 25-30cm to ensure a high number of laterals. Leaves are medium to large with rounded serration and a liberal scattering of fans. Tipping encourages prolific growth from lower laterals that quickly mature and move away from center but not too far for a Haze cross. Secondary development is profuse and gives the compact structure a very congested look. Upper laterals develop thickness in preparation for some oversized colas that will exceed human calf size with secondaries resembling tennis balls that are awash with resin. Indoors, large plants should reach approximately 50-60cm before inducing onset, as a gain of approximately 80-110% can be expected.

This variety is very well suited for multiple single stem setups, only requiring a short vegetation cycle after rooting, inducing onset at approximately 15-20cm. Haze #19 x Skunk#1 can produce some very serious colas that can be harvested at 56 days. This strain does not tolerate humidity and for indoor growers relative humidity would need to be kept below 65%. Keep EC levels low, flushing regularly and ensuring a two-week flush to finish.

Outdoor/greenhouse growers would need an arid climate or environmental control to succeed with this variety, but what results they would be. Using tipping and/or tying down with the extended vegetation cycle this plant's yield can be staggering. The secondaries are central to this plant's yield potential of high calyx to leaf ratio, primo herb. It is vital to select the correct phenotype: any that have typical Haze big gaps between nodal points and have budding sites that are widely staggered with Haze's speed of growth are wrong; the correct choice will have excessive results consistently of what I regard as my favorite 'all-rounder.' This strain is a true champion from Homegrown Fantaseeds.

AROMA, TASTE AND EFFECT

This strain is overwhelming in all departments. The fragrance in a growing plant is alcoholic; when lights come on there is a distinct fermenting alcohol aroma in the air. When a bud is cut a full-bodied fruit cocktail aroma with skunky undertones permeates the air—no sealed bag can contain this fragrance. The flavor is musky fruit, very pleasant and defining. The exhale leaves the palate with an aftertaste that lingers. The effect is very sedative and very immediate and should only be used at the end of the day or weekends. When buds have been dried over four weeks in the dark, the effect is trippy and very long lasting, with no ceiling level. My pulse rises when I reach for this jar!

HEAVY DUTY FRUITY

FLOWER PERIOD: 56-63 days
APPROX. FINISHED ON-SET HEIGHT: 85-110%
MAXIMUM RELATIVE HUMIDITY: 75%

MAXIMUM TDS / EC: 1.4 / **CF:** 14 / **PPM:** 980
3 x 400 WATT x 25cm POT / **YIELD** = 95gms+

From the start this strain is a moderate grower developing staggered nodal points. This usually determines format and in this case it means fewer laterals moving away from the center, opening the structure up and allowing good light access to the profuse secondary development. For large plant setups, tipping at approximately 25-30cm will ensure a good number of laterals. This variety needs a 24-hour light cycle through vegetation to offset pre-flowering. It has a big leaf format so trimming some offending leaf blades across their width will help give otherwise sheltered buds access to light.

When onset induced, approximately 50-60cm for big plant setups, an increase of approximately 85-110% can be expected. This strain has good resistance to mold, tolerating relative humidity of 75% and possibly higher. Nevertheless, I would recommend indoor growers who can control their environment do so, as a missed dead leaf in these very large colas would be trouble.

This is a top performer in multiple single stem setups requiring little vegetation time after rooting, inducing onset at approximately 15-20cm. Greenhouse/outdoor growers with an extended vegetation period should finish with a powerhouse of a plant using single stem, tipping and/or tying down. Just be aware of cola bud size if wet conditions are continuous nearing Heavy Duty Fruity finish. High calyx to leaf ratio makes manicuring quick work as the smaller leaves 'fold' with resin coverage. Keep EC levels low, flushing regularly and allowing a two-week flush to finish. This is a serious yielder in any setup.

AROMA, TASTE AND EFFECT

Heavy Duty Fruity has a strong fruity aroma when cut, a cocktail of apples, pears and peaches, a real fruit bouquet. Amazingly, it fails to transition to taste, but do not let this deter you. The taste is exotic, leaning toward the taste of hashy dates, and really rich and palatable. The effect is cerebral at first but uplifting with strength, encouraging a social response or outgoing pursuits until a delayed reaction 'leads the legs' and you look for a seat. This effect is of a long duration and ideal for long breaks between tokes. Cones are quite different, having no delay to the sedation. This is excellent for unwinding with at the end of the day or on evenings in.

HINDU KUSH

FLOWER PERIOD: 49-56 days
APPROX. FINISHED ON-SET HEIGHT: 50-70%
MAXIMUM RELATIVE HUMIDITY: 80%

MAXIMUM TDS / EC: 1.4 / CF: 14 / PPM: 980
3 x 400 WATT x 25cm POT / YIELD = 85gms+
MAXIMUM RESIN PRODUCTION AT 49 DAYS

Hindu Kush is a well-documented and established classic. One of the Afghan strains that stays short and stocky, this plant possesses many large fan leaves, so cutting across the width of some leaf blades will be required to allow light access to some hidden budding sites. This is another slow grower producing closely staggered nodal points that ensure a profuse development of laterals for large plant setups. No tipping is required, as the structure is extremely compact and crowded. This model was tipped for research and reflected a severe compromise to yield compared with a single stem version. When Hindu Kush is well established a profuse development of laterals move away from center, maturing with secondaries developing to give a very compact congested format.

Due to slow pace of growth even through onset, for large indoor plants ensure a good size of approximately 50-60cm+ before inducing onset as a gain of approximately 50-70% can be expected. Alternatively, take cuttings from a mother one week into onset, engaging lateral growth immediately after rooting, developing a multi-limbed open format plant from the start and retaining the center stem. Multiple single stem setups would require extra vegetation time, allowing cuttings to reach approximately 20-25cm before inducing onset. Pre-flowering begins after maturity through vegetation cycle (24-hour cycle required to offset) giving Hindu Kush a very quick response to onset, and by start of week five buds are very swollen and resin production is fierce.

Keep EC levels low and flush regularly, ensuring a two-week flush to finish. By 49 days Hindu Kush can be forearm-sized. If allowed to finish at 56 days, there is a noticeable increase in yield and the colas/buds take on a 'melt' look resembling toffee apples! Hindu Kush has a high calyx to leaf ratio and after drying (preferably four weeks in the dark) there is virtually no manicuring needed.

Excellent resistance to mold, tolerating relative humidity of 80%. Outdoor/greenhouse growers will have excellent results, with an even higher potency and flavor. Extended vegetation cycle and tying down will return excessive yields. The first Hindu Kush I grew was under a row of three x 400 watt lights, shared with 11 other plants, the Hindu Kush was approximately 150cm finished onset height, single stemmed, tied down and returned 140gms! Hindu Kush is in the upper echelons of this industry's varieties.

AROMA, TASTE AND EFFECT

When cut this bud has an aroma that seems almost turpentine-based. The mix in the bowl (held at an angle) when you run the scissors through it, melts back into the groove. The taste is a smooth hash with undertones of seasonings: oregano, thyme and marjoram to the exhale, and leaving the palate with a strong savory aftertaste. The effect is sedative over an extensive period of time with no ceiling level, excellent for long breaks between tokes or at the end of the day to unwind. Hindu Kush is a very powerful herb, so toke accordingly.

ICE

FLOWER PERIOD: 56-63 days
APPROX. FINISHED ON-SET HEIGHT: 100-130%
MAXIMUM RELATIVE HUMIDITY: 80%

MAXIMUM TDS / EC: 1.4 / CF: 14 / PPM: 980
3 x 600 WATT x 25cm POT / YIELD = 140gms+

A very fast-paced grower after rooting, Ice produces closely staggered nodal points producing a volume of laterals later in life or if tipped. Leaves are medium to large and dark green, other than the bud leaves; the count is minimal allowing light to access most budding sites. Tipping in a large plant setup should commence when Ice reaches approximately 25-30cm, producing a significant volume of laterals and secondaries that do not overly stray from center and giving the plant a crowded canopy which is where the low leaf count plays an important factor.

For big plant setups, allow Ice to reach at least 50-60cm before inducing onset as a gain of approximately 100-130% can be expected. Tying down is a necessity during this growth surge, although after two or three crops the grower will be able to precisely judge finished onset height and grow accordingly.

Flower early if height is a problem, inducing onset at 20-25cm together with a tipping. This allows for more plants, due to their finished size and tower format. Multiple single stem setups would only have to get cutting rooted, and after 4-7 days or approximately 15-20cm, induce onset for a very impressive stem. This strain exhibits excellent resistance to mold, tolerating relative humidity of 80% although the colas get extremely dense and large, so keep your eyes open for a dead leaf in a cola and remove it immediately if environmental control is not possible. All the same, for indoor growers who can control their environment, do so as standard practice and try to keep your room below 65% at all times. Low EC Levels with regular flushing will see the best from this strain ensuring a two-week flush to finish.

This is excellent for outdoor and greenhouse setups with its very good mold resistance and extended vegetation cycle; the returns are not only excessive but also produce one of the best quality herbs available. This strain is very versatile and in any format the yield is excessive without compromising quality.

AROMA, TASTE AND EFFECT

The aroma of Ice is as described by the seed bank, like that of high quality Nepali Hash, a wildflower floral fragrance. The taste transitions so well you can imagine sitting in the Himalayan Coffee House on Durbar Square in Kathmandu as you experience it, although when coned, the flavor is certainly fueled with hashy undertones. This is a rare ride into the Far East and the effect is quality, folding the mind with a series of effects followed by clarity and razor-sharp perceptions that imbue you with a personal confidence and well-being. Just as with hash, one's mindset is central to Ice's effect; it is a heavy cerebral delivery that can elevate creativity, and enhance museum or gallery visits and social interaction. It is a fine line between this effect and a full-on anesthetic delivery capable of knocking over any high tolerance tokers with no ceiling level and able to come over the top of anything. With a long duration getting more potent before an unnoticeable taper off, Ice is in a league of its own.

CURED BUD

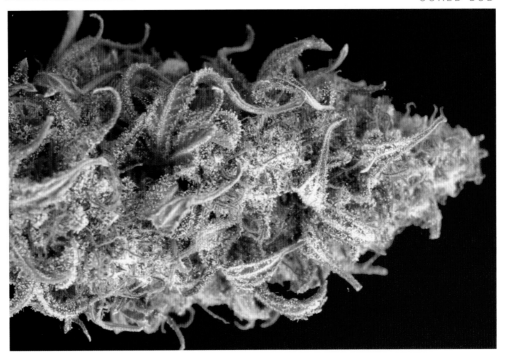

CURED BUD/CLOSEUP

REFLECTION +

This subject is of great importance for finding a cost-effective way of retaining escaping light and throwing it back into the garden. Yield increases in some cases of only a little increase in reflection can be staggering. These results for little outlay make this one of the prime bargains for the grower to get full potential from lighting. There are a variety of products available. Plastic material of usually varying grades of thickness, black on one side and white on the other, is good and has been used successfully and continually by indoor growers enforcing its establishment within the industry as a very fine product. Another product has a silver/foil-like material with an uneven surface to improve its reflective qualities. It's attached to a material similar to that used on house 'For Sale' signs (corrugated plastic), and generally sold in sheets of 900mm x 1200mm that can be cut to size easily with a cutting knife.

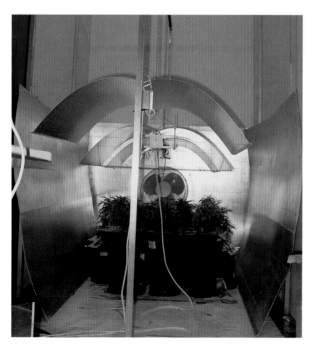

Use props like walls or chairs to angle the reflective board out from the base of the pots and support the lightweight panels. Ideally, the position of the top of the panel should be higher than the peripheral light that comes from under the shade. The panels are big enough to accommodate this requirement in most setups.

Angling reflection throws a greater amount of light back into the garden than flat hanging reflection.

A fan should be pushing air off the bulbs from one end of the garden through to the open end of the garden, keeping temperatures much lower for the plants and allowing a closer distance to plant tops. The look is a garden enclosed with angled reflective paneling, and the intensity will astound growers who have not previously utilized reflection efficiently and soon realize how much light was being lost. Sunglasses are best donned under these conditions; a few years without protection and you may incur a few problems of your own.

Another cheap and effective tip is to cover tops of pots with a sheet of foil. Tear a length that will cover the top of the pot and cut a slot in the foil to the center point so it can be slotted round the stem. The foil becomes a lid or cap and reflects directly back up under the leaves and lower stems and makes a significant difference in the growth stage particularly at a young age. Caps also prevent any algae growth on medium surfaces, encouraging roots to come to the surface as well as their usual travel. The prevention of algae growth allows oxygen a free unobstructed passage to the roots.

Rockwool cubes can be capped and this also prevents any algae forming, leaving the tops of cubes like the day you put them in. Roots get oxygen and grow out the top as well as the usual formation. The result is an abundance of newly formed root growth in cuttings and young plants, with very quick advances in growth cycle.

Foil caps on this mixed crop of Cinderella 99, Ultimate Indica, American Dream, Chronic, G13 and Bubblegum really advance growth at the base, developing as quickly as the growth under the bulb. This crop is between 25-30cm, all but the Ultimate Indica (taken from a mother kept in 24-hour) were taken from mothers one week into onset (mothers from previous crop). They will need to reach 50-60cm before inducing onset for this particular setup.

LEDA UNO

FLOWER PERIOD: 56-63 days
APPROX. FINISHED ON-SET HEIGHT: 60-80%
MAXIMUM RELATIVE HUMIDITY: 65%

MAXIMUM TDS / EC: 1.4 / CF: 14 / PPM: 980
3 x 600 WATT x 25cm POT / YIELD = 145gms+

The plant modelled is the short version; there are two phenotypes of this strain and for indoor purposes the shorter version was selected. Correct selection for indoor setups is vital to achieve the results set out here. This is a slow-paced grower that produces many closely staggered nodal points off the main stem ensuring a proliferation of lateral development later in vegetation cycle. Do not tip Leda Uno as this compromises yield. For large plant setups take cuttings from mothers one week into onset. This immediately engages lateral growth after rooting and retains a single stem format, enabling all-round growth from the start, achieving a very mature structure early in life.

For big plants setups ensure a good size is achieved before inducing onset, 50-60cm as a gain of approximately 60-80% can be expected by the start of week 4. Budding sites are very closely staggered locking up from midway point to produce excessive colas. This variety is susceptible to mold so keep relative humidity below 65% and ideally below 60% starting week six if possible. Keep EC levels low, flushing regularly and allow a two-week flush to finish.

Multiple single stem setups would require extra vegetation time so allow cuttings to reach approximately 20-25cm before inducing onset. By 56 days it is hard to believe there could be any increases but taken to 63 days there is a noticeable increase accompanied by a color spectrum that will captivate you. A high calyx to leaf ratio means very little manicuring, as resin adorns high-calyx-to-leaf-ratio colas, the center one consistently forearm-sized and the secondaries sometimes resembling tennis balls! Greenhouse/outdoor growers will require an arid climate or have environmental control due to Leda's susceptibility to mold. However the returns should be staggering with the extended vegetation period; tying down will be necessary to keep plants hidden and amazingly increase yield capability. This is a mammoth of a plant that is an adrenaline rush to grow.

AROMA, TASTE AND EFFECT

Leda Uno's fragrance has been described as 'lemon drop' and I agree with this. When the bud is cut the mouth will water, such is the aroma, and the taste transitions superbly well, like a boiled sweet. The exhale is accompanied with a slight earthiness to the drop that leaves with the smoke. The palate is left feeling very refreshed. The effect is cerebrally heavy, thoughts linger, you find yourself staring while thinking. The body is eased into relaxation rather than jolted. It is excellent for conversing or winding down at the end of the day. That said, I didn't find chillin' difficult with Leda Uno, while at the same time it was excellent to go to bed on. Versatility adds another appealing aspect to this high-quality champion.

CURED BUD

CURED BUD/CLOSEUP

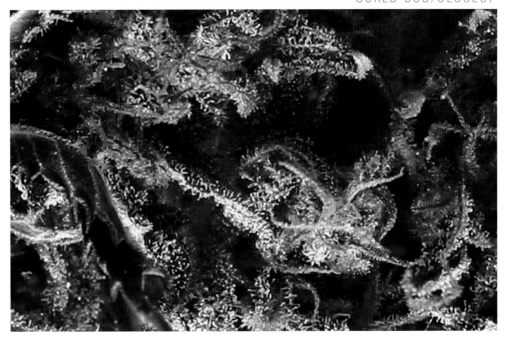

MAZAR

FLOWER PERIOD: 63 days
APPROX. FINISHED ON-SET HEIGHT: 100-120%
MAXIMUM RELATIVE HUMIDITY: 75%

MAXIMUM TDS / EC: 1.4 / CF: 14 / PPM: 980
3 x 600 WATT x 25cm POT / YIELD = 125gms+

Mazar grows at a fast pace, forming staggered, distanced nodal points up the stem ensuring Mazar's format is an open structure, producing fewer laterals that quickly move away from center and can develop to their full potential due to not being overcrowded. Leaves are few, medium to large and remaining dark green to finish. Tipping for large plant setups at approximately 25-30cm produces a higher number of laterals. Inducing onset at approximately 50-60cm will result in a gain of approximately 100-120%; tying down will facilitate maximum yield potential by keeping the development of budding sites close due to horizontal position of laterals and main stems.

In multiple single stem setups, Mazar would require little vegetation time after rooting, allowing cutting to reach 15-20cm before inducing onset. For personal growers with height restrictions and unable to use multiple single stem setup, induce onset at approximately 20-25cm with a tipping, or alternatively, take cuttings from a mother one week into onset to engage lateral growth immediately after striking, ensuring that a very open structure develops from the start and the plant reaches a very advanced, mature format at 25cm. Keep EC levels low and flush weekly ensuring a two-week flush to finish. Budding sites are staggered till growth slows, then they begin to lock up to produce long, dense colas and golf-ball-size secondaries. Mazar has good resistance to mold, tolerating indoor relative humidity of 75% and possibly a little higher.

Outdoor/greenhouse setups should have very good results using tying down due to extended vegetation cycle. This plant can be grown in most setups with good success. The buds have a distinct Sativa appearance to them and begin hardening and producing resin at start of week seven. Finished at 63 days, Mazar buds are of a very high calyx to leaf ratio and extremely dense. After drying in the dark for four weeks there will be so little leaf to remove this strain is possibly one of the fastest to manicure, which is a very significant purchasing factor.

AROMA, TASTE AND EFFECT

Mazar's aroma when cut is of dried fruit (prunes, raisins, figs, dates); an overwhelming sense of Middle Eastern delights greets the nose, rich and mystical with body. The fragrance transitions to taste well. A menagerie of dried fruit with subtle sweet aniseed undertones to the exhale makes this the perfect smoke after dinner, neutralizing the palate of any lingering post-dinner aftertastes, particularly as the effect is dynamically euphoric, uplifting, and prolonged, encouraging social pursuits or activity. The buds have an appearance like glasses of sparkling champagne. This strain is excellent after breakfast with coffee.

MAZAR I-SHARIF

FLOWER PERIOD: 56-63 days
APPROX. FINISHED ON-SET HEIGHT: 60-80%
MAXIMUM RELATIVE HUMIDITY: 75%

MAXIMUM TDS / EC: 1.4 / CF: 14 / PPM: 980
3 x 600 WATT x 25cm POT / YIELD = 130gms+

This is another slow-paced grower producing closely staggered nodal points that will produce a high number of laterals giving the plant a compact, congested structure later in life. For big plant setups allow Mazar i-Sharif to grow as a single stem, as tipping a mature plant can compromise yield. Single stem versions consistently produce an oversized center stem, other tipped copies have been inconsistent in developing this format.

In big plant setups ensure a good size is reached, approximately 50-60cm when onset induced as an overall gain of approximately 60-80% can be expected. Keep EC levels low and flush once per week ensuring a two-week flush to finish. Multiple single stem setups will require extra vegetation time after rooting, inducing onset at approximately 20-25cm. This plant responds to onset slowly with stigmas turning purple at week four; hardening and resin production begin at start of week six. Winding down the lights-off hours from 35 days by 30 minutes per week to the finish 56 days may hasten buds to finish harder with even more resin but observe for abnormalities and cease if hermaphroditing occurs. Personal growers may want to harvest 63 days just to ensure the complete finish.

This strain has good resistance to mold and can tolerate relative humidity up to 75%, which is aided by the structure of the buds. Watch for dead or dying leaves, removing immediately. Greenhouse/outdoor growers will have very good results, extended vegetation cycle and tying should see excessive yielding. This variety is an awe inspiring experience to be involved with and watch develop.

AROMA, TASTE AND EFFECT

The aroma from a cut bud is citrus/lemon, a light refreshing zest surrounds you. The taste is richly different, reflecting figs/dates with hashy undertones allowing the palate to linger over a long lasting flavor that is richly satisfying. The effect is very euphoric and uplifting. This one is excellent any time of the day, but particularly with coffee after breakfast to really fire up the noggin.

CURED BUD

CURED BUD/CLOSEUP

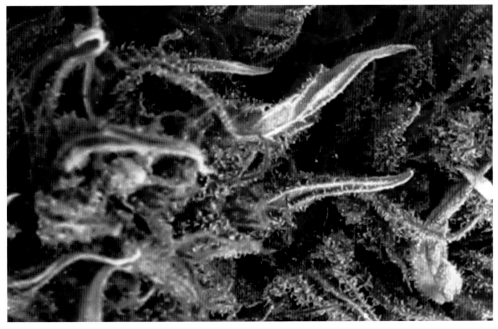

MEDICINE MAN

FLOWER PERIOD: 49-56 days
APPROX. FINISHED ON-SET HEIGHT: 50-70%
MAXIMUM RELATIVE HUMIDITY: 75%

MAXIMUM TDS / EC: 1.4 / CF: 14 / PPM: 980
3 x 400 WATT x 25cm POT / YIELD = 90gms+
MAXIMUM RESIN PRODUCTION AT 49 DAYS

Medicine Man grows slowly, forming many closely staggered nodal points ensuring a proliferation of laterals later in life or if tipped. In large plant setups tipping a plant at approximately 25-30cm will ensure a high number of laterals that mature and slowly move away form center, opening Medicine Man up and allowing light good access to all budding sites. Apart from leaves that surround the buds, Medicine Man produces few medium-to-fan-sized leaves that remain a dark green throughout life cycle.

For a large plant setup ensure the plant is of good size, approximately 50-60cm as inducement of onset produces an overall gain of approximately 50-70%. In a multiple single stem setup extra vegetation time will be necessary after rooting, allowing cutting to reach 20-25cm before inducing onset for some excessive colas. Low EC rates must be adhered to along with regular flushing and ensuring a two-week flush to finish. This strain has excellent mold resistance, tolerating humidity up to 75%; all the same, if you can control your environment then do so, as even with resistant plants accidents can happen.

For outdoor/greenhouse growers this plant's resistance to high humidity is welcome news but Medicine man is not impervious to mold. With extended vegetation period and tipping, Medicine Man can be managed to have the appearance of a truncated tree and the short flower cycle should keep Medicine Man ahead of seasonal change and aid when drying. The resin production and bud size at 49 days will have indoor growers comparing forearms; let it run to the 56 days for even more resin, a noticeable increase in yield, and colas that resemble Popeye's arms! Medicine Man can be harvested at 49 days with a finished look in excess of most other varieties.

AROMA, TASTE AND EFFECT

The aroma when cutting the bud is very powerful, aromatic seasonings like thyme and oregano with subtle undertones of aniseed erupt, making a complex fragrance. The taste transitions well; the heat brings out the strong seasoning flavor and on the exhale I even detected an underlying subtle mint in the taste. This complex flavor is excellent to debate with others. The effect is potent, medicinal strength that leaves you debilitated; it will erase any 'post-toke' plans outside of a 'play' button. There is no ceiling level and the effect increases over an extensive duration with an unnoticeable taper off.

CURED BUD

BIO-PONIC/ORGANIC +

For this grow I selected a coco-coir medium as a lot of good information had accompanied this product and I like to try different ideas out of interest. I used clay balls at the bottom of 25cm pots to a depth of approximately 5cm then filled with the coco-coir. Through the 12-hour flower cycle, I fed with a range of organic nutrients from the shelf and a high quality enzyme product with every feed to ensure a strong, healthy micro-life that protected and provided the perfect growing environment.

The plants grew very well, not as fast as hydroponic but certainly not lacking. Pots can be watered individually or a delivery system installed. Hand-watered and non-return automatic delivery systems do not spread disease or infection through watering as a hydroponic setup can. Any problems normally stay isolated within each pot. Pots are easy to move around which is handy for a mixed garden of Indicas and Sativas.

Soil does seem to attract flies in the form of the fungus gnat family—fruit flies and scarid flies. The soil and bacteria micro life act as a buffer to the disease, not the insect. They do need to be controlled though as a warm to hot environment without air-conditioning will encourage proliferation and irritation. Sticky fly traps are extremely effective and placed on top of pots and on the floor as well as hanging, soon fill up and have to be replaced in some situations. Cooler temperatures that air-conditioning provides or basement gardens below 25°C are disliked by these particular flies and although it will not eradicate them completely it does reduce the proliferation drastically. Grease halfway along the inside of the saucer lip (so as not to contaminate run-off) with petroleum jelly, and this acts as a sticky fly trap and catches all the

new flightless scarids from spreading to the next pot. Although this will not affect the flying ones the chain is being halted at hatchling level in severe cases.

Soil or dirt is a lot more forgiving than a hydroponic setup and will allow a pot to almost dry without a serious setback. Wet soil through the dark period will raise humidity, so always try to water when lights come on, allowing any excess to be used by the plant over the daylight cycle with evaporation leaving pots with a patchy or dry top surface to go through the dark period. (This applies where setups are not utilizing environmental controls like air-conditioning or dehumidifiers.)

Plants go through a very natural color change from the strong greens of growth through a menagerie of colors when flowering, especially when using organic feed. Flavors are pronounced and last longer when burning. The effect is uncompromisingly clean.

Afghan X Skunk showing an array of colors.

NORTHERN LIGHTS #5 X HAZE #19

FLOWER PERIOD: 84 days
APPROX. FINISHED ON-SET HEIGHT: 100-130%
MAXIMUM RELATIVE HUMIDITY: 80%

MAXIMUM TDS / EC: 1.4 / CF: 14 / PPM: 980
3 x 400 WATT x 25cm POT / YIELD = 95gms+

This variety takes patience but the return is dynamic. It's a fast-paced grower, particularly when maturity is reached, with medium-sized leaves and a scattering of fans with round serrations. Nodal points are widely staggered suggesting fewer laterals that will quickly move away from center opening the format up after the plant is well matured. Inducing onset at approximately 50-60cm will result in four weeks of prolific growth, with the Northern Lights parentage unable to intervene. Expect a gain of approximately 100-130%, mainly vertical, and in big plant setups, tying down has to be applied to control height and keep budding sites close, maximizing yield potential.

Alternatively, flowering early approximately 20-25cm will be appropriate where height is restricted, however, tipping will compromise yield, as model used here reflects (tipped for research). Northern Lights does not respond well to tipping and many crosses using Northern Lights seem to perform better as a single stem. Tying down single stem plant will return a substantial yield and you'll want that after patiently waiting 12 weeks. Multiple single stem setups will require little vegetation time after rooting, allowing cutting to reach 15-20cm before inducing onset. At eight weeks the buds are still hairy and white.

Low EC rates are recommended for best results: flush every week, stopping feed altogether at week nine and flushing to the finish. Outdoor/greenhouse growers should reap excellent results with extended vegetation cycle and good mold resistance, although the colas can get oversized and if unexpected prolonged wet climate ensues nearing finish, it will be safer to harvest a little earlier. This strain has excellent resistance to mold indoors as well, tolerating indoor humidity up to 80%, and can probably tolerate a few notches higher. This is needed due to long flower cycle, which produces one of the most potent varieties I have tested.

To encourage a slightly quicker finish the dark period can be wound down from 42 days by 30 minutes per week for four weeks and by 70 days you may want to harvest—it's your decision. Watch for abnormalities when winding down as some varieties can go hermaphrodite. Really, this one is for growers seeking the high that lasts and folds the mind into many different layers. If you have the patience this variety will bring to you very impressive yields of extremely potent herb.

AROMA, TASTE AND EFFECT

I find the aroma to be extremely pungent and bold, a mixture of fermenting beer and mature cheese! It is wickedly heavy on the nose. As delightful as this sounds, sadly it does not transition to taste but do not let that diminish your excitement, as the flavor is very hashy with an earthiness, and the palate is left to savour wonderful hashy overtones. If dried correctly and cured, this herb is like Cognac, smooth and flavorful with an effect that will be among the best you've experienced. The effect is totally sedative, immediate and for an extensive period of time with no ceiling level and very capable of coming over the top of any other herb. It's truly potent.

SENSI STAR

FLOWER PERIOD: 49-56 days
APPROX. FINISHED ON-SET HEIGHT: 50-70%
MAXIMUM RELATIVE HUMIDITY: 75%

MAXIMUM TDS / EC: 1.4 / CF: 14 / PPM: 980
3 x 400 WATT x 25cm POT / YIELD = 90gms+
MAXIMUM RESIN PRODUCTION AT 49 DAYS

This is one of the strains responsible for setting the standard of Indicas on the market today and it still holds its place among the best Indicas available. Sensi Star is easy to clone and grows slowly throughout the vegetation cycle producing closely staggered nodal points that ensure a proliferation of laterals later in life or if tipped. Large plant setups should tip Sensi Star at approximately 25-30cm to ensure a good volume of laterals that will mature and slowly move away from center opening Sensi Star up and allowing light good access to all budding sites. The closeness of budding sites, combined with their size, means every lateral becomes congested with development. Apart from small leaves around buds which will literally drip resin, there are very few medium sized leaves on Sensi Star.

Ensure a good size, approximately 50-60cm, has been established when inducing onset for a large plant as an overall gain of 50-70% can be expected. In a multiple single stem setup Sensi Star will require extra vegetation time, allowing the cuttings to reach 20-25cms before inducing onset. Resin production is extreme by 35 days, coupled with hardening and still with two to three weeks to finish!

A heavy yielder that performs best with low levels of EC as is the case with most, if not all plants, flushing regularly and ensuring a two-week flush to finish is advised for the best results. It has excellent resistance to mold, tolerating relative humidity of 75%. Keep a watchful eye for dead leaves if this figure cannot be reduced; for growers who can control their environment, keep below 65% relative humidity as standard practice.

Outdoor/greenhouse growers will excel with Sensi Star using extended vegetation cycle and tipping, and the yields can be excessive. The short flower cycle should keep it ahead of seasonal change and aid with drying. This is a versatile and exceptional variety with a very high calyx to leaf ratio making virtually no manicuring necessary after drying and resin production that can be equaled by very few (only six others in this book). Sensi Star is very capable of producing forearms for colas and golf balls for secondaries by 49 days, however if allowed to finish 56 days, they become excessive and captivating with absolutely no trim; from the dirt up every nug has density where good reflection is used.

AROMA, TASTE AND EFFECT

Sensi Star has quite an individual aroma in that it is extremely savory. When cutting, I can smell a casserole cooking on the stove, real meat and potatoes with a seasoning of oregano, thyme and marjoram. The flavor is quite different, exotic tastes of Middle Eastern delights, dates, and figs, with good body as the palate is left with a delightfully rich aftertaste. The effect is of medicinal strength with an immediate cerebral delivery that will extinguish every thought. The body becomes very relaxed and there is no ceiling when indulging. The effect is prolonged and can encourage sleep unless preoccupied. This is extremely potent herb with the ability to come over the top of most other varieties.

CURED BUD

CURED BUD/CLOSEUP

YIELD INCREASING TECHNIQUES
OFF-SETTING VERTICAL GROWTH

GROW ROOM NOTES +

This is a topic of interest for myself, and through helpful publications, and the many varieties, I have been able to grow Indica-dominant strains side by side with Sativa-dominant strains in a confined area. These are a few already established methods used in the horticultural industry for increasing yield factor and controlling vertical height at the same time.

SUPERCROPPING

Supercropping is useful in dealing with plants with Sativa-dominant characteristics, or plants that need to be slowed down because they are growing too far in advance of others, in order to allow for a more even canopy and even light dispersal. When applying supercropping to young seedlings or cuttings, allow them to reach approximately

20-25cm before first treatment. In the case of multiple single stem setups, this would coincide with onset inducement for Indica-dominant strains. However, for Sativa-dominant strains having onset induced at 15-20cm, this is the only time super cropping should be initiated this early.

The procedure, due to soft stems, involves a gentle squeeze between thumb and index finger; only a little pressure will be required before a crack is heard or felt, or the stem softens, but avoid compressing the stem altogether. Correctly treated the plant can either remain upright or sag over when the procedure is finished. If cuttings sag over, no problem as they will return to a vertical position over a few days to one week, while reinforcement of the stem takes place. For treatments to large established plants, the procedure changes and even secondaries can be mature

enough to require more work than a squeeze can achieve. Take the lateral or secondary and gently roll the stem between your index finger and thumb, adding a slight amount of pressure. After rolling the stem several times, it will soften but the surface will not break. Roll until the head rotates three quarters of a full turn, and then gently back the other way. Start low down the stem, try to avoid crushing, and if nodal sites are too close start further up. If the plant is young it is easy to rotate the stem too far and the head snaps clean off, but it does not take long to get the technique right. Up the main stem apply treatment at equal distances, approximately 2cm. The stems can sag over as if they've been denied water; this is the finished look of supercropping. After 24-72 hours they should be vertical again and then the plant will focus on repairing the damage internally and reinforcing the damaged area to ensure this injury does not reoccur. This work will halt the plant's growth for three to seven days depending on the thoroughness of the treatment.

The technique changes on the second treatment as the plant has matured and the stem has thickened from the first

A successfully supercropped stem can deliver vast amounts of feed to colas.

All that you see here comes from the stem pictured above of a supercropped Bubbleberry in a 600w flood 'n drain system. It is bigger than it looks! An absolute leviathan. Photo credit Smutly.

treatment. This time a better grip is required and a bit more grunt. Taking mature plant in a firm grip between index finger and thumb, using both hands turn gently in opposite directions until a chiropractic crack can be heard or felt between the fingers; if you hear that sound, you've successfully damaged the inner hurd without damaging the outer stem. If there is no crack but the stem has been rotated, the process is still successful as the hurd cannot remain intact when opposing forces are applied to the stems. Depending on the strain and maturity of the plant, there maybe some work for a thorough job.

Take your time and be fully focused on your job or accidents will happen. It is best to remove the plant from the crop to work on comfortably as even the biggest plants I have worked on can take approximately 30-60 minutes. The end result is larger stems, allowing the plant to absorb greater volumes of water more quickly than with standard stems, and this is reflected in substantial increases in yields.

It does not take long to familiarize yourself with this technique and the results can be astounding. Do not supercrop a plant more than three times, and allow for a good recovery before each treatment; try not to go back over areas already treated, always treat new growth only. First treatment should be at approximately 25-30cm and the last at the inducement of onset. Do not apply later than the start of second week of onset as this may delay budding.

TIPPING

Tipping can be basic or complex depending on the grower and what strains he or she may have. If tipping is part of your grow plan, the first tipping is normally performed on the one central growing stem. Wait till the plant is approximately 20-25cm, as this ensures a good number of laterals below the cut. When the plant reaches 50-60cm a second tipping treatment can be applied to encourage even more secondary development and in most cases, with extended vegetation cycle, yield potential is dramatically increased.

For tipping, a plant should be mature, approximately 25-30cm minimum acceptable height; the top of the main stem, or head, is removed. The cut is made on the stem halfway between the head to be removed and the next nodal point. The plant panics and responds by initiating lateral and secondary development, which invariably results in a number of laterals producing comparable-sized colas to a single stem version. However, there are a few cases, but not many, where tipping is advised against as it actually diminishes the large size some colas and secondaries can get to as a single stemmed plant. With experience, using this method on standard-sized plants (one or two treatments) or big plants (two or three treatments) will substantially increase the yield potential.

TIE DOWN

This method is used to keep fast-growing plants under control and maximize their yield; using fewer plants and extra vegetation period are required for this method to achieve substantial yield increases.

The principle is that in a given area where 12 plants under two x 400 watt could be grown there would instead be 6-8 pots. These should be strains with great growing potential, not Indica or predominately Indica crosses, which are unsuited to this technique for indoor purposes. (However tie down would be a necessity for greenhouse/outdoor setups regardless of strain, if height begins to exceed expectation due to long vegetation cycle.) Depending on growing setup, plants can be tied at any stage, purposely planned or in emergencies; it will only increase yield. Plants are tied down quite extremely, but be gentle taking the stems over. If rigid-

A prolific grower, at the fourth week of on-set, El Nino has been contained using a combination of early on-set, approx. 35cm height with a tipping treatment preventing new stems elongating. This format can be achieved on all tall varieties using these techniques.

Sativa dominant plants tied down.

ity is prevalent then lean the stems gradually, allowing a day between each stage until the stem is as low as possible, and tie off using canes or anchored sites.

As the heads turn upward and begin to grow and five to eight new nodes have formed, pull the lead head down again so that it is travelling horizontally, and the plants are trained around the open area of the garden. By the stem being exposed horizontally, the budding sites turn vertically toward the light and begin to develop a stem of their own and budding sites! By pulling the plant down you have taken away the leading stem primarily selected by the plant to be responsible for providing the biggest growth, to

ensure pollination by catching any pollen floating around. Suddenly the race is on to become the leading cola and this is contested by every budding site that evolves into colas. The production of stems is phenomenal. Do not be overwhelmed if yields are two to three times the quoted return.

LOWER STEM REMOVAL

Some growers like to keep the lower stems and use the lower buds, less developed due to lack of light, for kief or hashish. Others prefer to clear the main stems of lower laterals and secondaries and remove up to 50% from the dirt up, allowing good airflow through the bottom part of the garden and redirecting bud growth into the already established remaining stems, which results in bigger crowns and colas. Do not remove such large amounts any later than onset as the shock will disrupt the flower cycle. The plant must be young enough and have some vegetation growth left, ideally one week prior to onset, to allow time for recovery, including the four weeks of onset. When this process is performed correctly, a plant will display a canopy of colas with very little work involved regarding manicuring.

Lower stem removal – G13. Photo credit Smutly.

SENSI STAR X SHISHKABERRY

FLOWER PERIOD: 56-63 days
APPROX. FINISHED ON-SET HEIGHT: 80-100%
MAXIMUM RELATIVE HUMIDITY: 75%

MAXIMUM TDS / EC: 1.4 / CF: 14 / PPM: 980
3 x 400 WATT x 25cm POT / YIELD = 95gms+

This is a moderate-paced grower producing staggered nodal points off the main stem. Later in life or when tipped, the plant will exhibit fewer laterals, moving away from the center and opening it up with a profuse development of secondaries. In large plant setups, allow height to reach 25-30cm before tipping to promote a high number of laterals. Leaves are medium to large with a liberal scattering of fans. They have a round serration, and are dark green with a blue shimmer to the periphery of the blades, which remain this color to finish.

Inducing onset at approximately 50-60cm (large plant setups) will result in a gain of approximately 80-100% with a compact appearance. Multiple single stem setups will require little vegetation time after rooting; allow cuttings to reach 15-20cm before inducing onset. Quickest response to onset I have witnessed to date (as picture opposite indicates) was at three and a half weeks, revealing the potential resin production this plant is capable of. Secondaries are staggered up the stems prolifically while the buds on the main laterals lock up as growth slows through onset to produce very dense, forearm-plus, resin-dripping colas by 56 days. If allowed to run to 63 days, the colas become excessive. Watch for dying leaves and remove immediately.

Buds have a distinctive blue hue to them and are glazed with a Sensi Star finish guaranteed to induce a cough after tokes. Keep EC levels low and flush frequently ensuring a two-week flush to finish. This strain has good resistance to mold, tolerating a relative humidity of 75% and possibly a little higher.

Outdoor/greenhouse growers should excel with this variety using extended vegetation cycle. Sensi Star x Shishkaberry will need to be tied down and kept out of sight, and this cross should return bewildering yields—it's very successful in most setups and will quickly become a favorite; a real masterpiece.

AROMA, TASTE AND EFFECT

The fragrance of a cut bud is 'very berry,' indicative of the Shishkaberry parentage, which goes so well with the 'blue hue' buds' display. The taste transitions superbly with a sweet berry flavor, the exhale leaving a hashy aftertaste for the palate to savour with a berry influence; delightful. The effect is a mule kick to the head, the toker having the appearance of a 'stunned mullet,' the body relaxes and hours rolls by, courtesy of the Sensi Star's influence bringing no ceiling level and the ability to come over the top of most other herbs. This is very potent herb and must be dried over four weeks in the dark to achieve best results. Use in 'free time' only!

SHARK SHOCK

FLOWER PERIOD: 49-56 days
APPROX. FINISHED ON-SET HEIGHT: 100-130%
MAXIMUM RELATIVE HUMIDITY: 80%

MAXIMUM TDS / EC: 1.4 / CF: 14 / PPM: 980
3 x 400 WATT x 25cm POT / YIELD = 90gms+
MAXIMUM RESIN PRODUCTION AT 49 DAYS

This variety has a good yield potential, and clones strike with relative ease. It's a vigorous, robust plant that grows at a fast pace producing distanced staggered nodal points that later in life or when tipped develop fewer laterals that quickly move away from center but not enough to describe this as an open format. Laterals stay in close proximity of center and only the budding cycle forces them to open out extensively. In large plant setups allow Shark Shock to reach 25-30cm before tipping to facilitate in a high number of laterals. In multiple single stem setups Shark Shock will require little vegetation time after rooting, allowing cutting to reach approximately 15-20cm before inducing onset. Keep lights a minimum of one meter above cuttings to allow them to adjust to high lumens, lowering light approximately 15cm every fourth day until desired height is reached. Inducing onset sends a big plant into a prolific vertical growth pattern, with laterals extending with maturity and speed but still maintaining closely staggered bud formation.

Expect a vertical gain of approximately 100-130% by the end of the fourth week; tying down will be necessary in large plant setups. The leaves are large with a liberal scattering of fans that remain dark green through to finish. Keep EC levels low and flush regularly and ensure a two-week flush to finish for optimum results. Shark Shock resins up extremely early; the staggered budding sites lock up when onset slows to construct some very dense colas. High calyx to leaf ratio ensures little manicuring and the plant looks very finished at 49 days, literally spitting resin,

although taken to 56 days the plants will have a substantial increase in both factors.

Shark Shock withstands relative humidity of up to 80%, although the colas can get very large and dense so be watchful of dead leaves. Resin adorns the leaves causing them to fold with crystallization; even the base nugs are quality. For growers with height restrictions, try inducing onset at approximately 25cm and tip at the same time. Outdoor/greenhouse growers will have excellent results from this strain and particularly using the tie down method combined with short flower cycle, it should stay ahead of seasonal change. This is a big yielder by nature so any method of growing will give excellent returns.

AROMA, TASTE AND EFFECT

Shark Shock has an extremely pronounced aroma of epoxy glue when cut. It is a very striking fragrance that is powerfully dense and most people are overwhelmed. The aroma almost burns the nose, and the taste transitions extremely well and is not unlike a thinner flavor when exhaled, quite unusual and extremely pleasant. The effect is heavily sedative and quick especially if dried over four weeks in the dark. The head becomes heavy, as do thoughts; the body soon follows. The duration is long, making this ideal to smoke at the end of the day, evenings, or weekends.

SHISHKABERRY

FLOWER PERIOD: 56-63 days
APPROX. FINISHED ON-SET HEIGHT: 100-130%
MAXIMUM RELATIVE HUMIDITY: 75%

MAXIMUM TDS / EC: 1.4 / CF: 14 / PPM: 980
3 x 400 WATT x 25cm POT / YIELD = 95gms+

A fast-paced grower, Shishkaberry develops staggered nodal points that ensure a profuse development of laterals later in life or if tipped. In large plant setups, allow Shishkaberry to reach 25-30cm before tipping to facilitate in the growth of a high number of laterals that immediately move away from center, opening the format up. As they mature and establish, a prolific development of secondaries give the laterals a very congested look, creating a lattice between the limbs.

This variety does produce a bit more leaf but the colas and buds will distract your attention once the fifth week is under way. A mature Shishkaberry approximately 50-60cm in height at onset will gain approximately an extra 100-130% and will need to be tied down to allow full development. For personal growers with height restrictions and unable to use single stem setup, allow Shishkaberry to reach 20-25cm before inducing onset with a tipping to offset growth surge. In multiple single stem setups, Shishkaberry requires little vegetation time after rooting, allowing cutting to reach 15-20cm before inducing onset.

Keep EC levels low and flush regularly ensuring a two-week flush to finish for best results. The buds take on an expected blue hue coupled with excessive resin coverage by start of week seven. Shishkaberry has very good resistance to mold, tolerating relative humidity of 75%, although if no environmental control is used observe for dead or dying leaves and remove immediately. At 56 days buds and colas are very dense and appear white with resin coverage, and

these factors increase noticeably if taken to 63 days, becoming excessive. Growers with setups requiring extreme returns using fewer plants (good experience needed for maximum results using this method) will be very pleased with this purchase. Outdoor/greenhouse growers should excel with this variety, taking advantage of its mold resistance and high yield potential, particularly with the extended vegetation period and tying down.

AROMA, TASTE AND EFFECT

Shishkaberry finishes with an abundance of resin coverage and cutting into a bud that has been dried over four weeks in the dark releases a sweet berry aroma that is very pleasant and not overpowering. The transition to taste is excellent, leaving the palate with a berry hash aftertaste. The effect is sedative, with a heavy cerebral delivery that will halt thinking immediately with no ceiling level and an extensive taper off; excellent to unwind with at the end of the day or on evenings in.

DRYING THE HERB +

This area is the real make or break stage. Observe those that will, in their haste for the taste, microwave, fry, grill, bake, and dehydrate their herb. Speed drying is wreckless. Hanging it on racks and blowing air over the crop is not going to produce good grade bud. Sweating it up in a bag to draw out moisture removes most of the aromas and flavors.

The following method is the tried, trusted option of several available to the grower. Cut the plant into separate limbs, if plants are dense, allowing better airflow. Hang on whatever is most convenient—clotheslines to clothes racks—and do not remove any leaves whatsoever. Move air around the room; if drying in a cupboard/wardrobe, put a fan on the floor pointing away, not on the plants. The area should be kept cool and dark, though it doesn't have to be pitch-black.

After four weeks the buds are usually firm to stiff to the touch; when cut it should have the perfect soft, fluffy interior as it falls into your bowl. When stems snap (four weeks+) remove the remainder of insignificant leaves. However, very little manicuring should be required as the secondary leaves reduce so much they curl around the nugs, protecting the resin glands from harm.

El Nino

Large fan leaves should be noticeably reduced in size and crisp, so that they flick off; the rest are very resined and should remain, as resined leaves have a taste and sweetness different from that of the bud. Now they can be bagged or jarred.

After one week, open bags or jars on a good clear, sunny day (low humidity) and allow the herb to air for one day; then reseal for three months minimum (cure).

When dried over four weeks they really are down to the minimum retained moisture in the buds. I do open once per month for a nug as I like to analyze the cure and that allows fresh air in. Primo cured herb: it is as easy as that.

If storing in freezer, ensure herb is at the above stage. Wrap the herb in five to six separate sheets of clear film. Take the parcel and place inside a plastic shopping bag, repeating this also five to six times in order to eliminate as much air from each bag as possible. This can now be placed in the freezer and enjoyed up to two years. I personally tried this and it was the longest I had stored it for and the aroma was kicking through as I reached the clear film. Taste and fragrance were unimpaired from the cryogenic experience, as was the effect, although it was not as smooth as cured herb. The herb is as it was the day it went in. Within three weeks it changed from the fresh light green it came out as, to cured khaki, and smoothness improved dramatically.

Should herb be overdried or just dried due to time, a fresh green leaf can be placed into bag or jar with it and over 24 hours the herb will become softer.

After four weeks drying, herb is now bagged and awaiting inspection.

Clothes racks work very well as do lines.

SHIVA SKUNK

FLOWER PERIOD: 49-56 days
APPROX. FINISHED ON-SET HEIGHT: 100-130%
MAXIMUM RELATIVE HUMIDITY: 75%

MAXIMUM TDS / EC: 1.4 / CF: 14 / PPM: 980
3 x 600 WATT x 25cm POT / YIELD = 140gms+

Shiva Skunk grows at a moderate pace; development of nodal points is staggered, ensuring when Shiva Skunk is well established lateral development will quickly move away from center, opening the structure up and allowing light to access the profuse development of secondaries that give Shiva Skunk a very busy, congested appearance. Shiva Skunk's yield will be compromised if tipped (reflected in the model shown—tipped for research) and is far better to leave as a single stem. Leaves are medium to large with a rounded serration, remaining a dark green throughout its cycle, with only a few fading near the finish.

Shiva reacts quickly to onset: within two days Shiva Skunk begins to show signs of a growth frenzy as nodal points stretch along with budding sites. Tying down is the best way of controlling Shiva Skunk, maximizing yield and keeping budding sites close due to horizontal format. The other option if height is a problem is to flower early at approximately 20-25cm (depending on height restrictions). Shiva is excellent for multiple single stem setups, requiring little vegetation time after rooting, inducing onset at approximately 15-20cm, and producing impressive high calyx to leaf colas.

When newly rooted cuttings are placed into main setup, remember to keep lights at least a meter high to avoid stress from high lumens, and reduce approximately 10-15cm every fourth day until sufficient. Inducing onset on a mature plant of 50-60cm will result in a 100-130% vertical gain. Shiva Skunk's quick reaction time to onset means buds and colas have quite an advanced look by start of week six, with hardening and resin production. I found harvesting Shiva Skunk at 49 days with a four-week dry was aromatic, flavorsome and produced a reasonable high. If allowed to flower till 56 days, these factors are noticeably elevated as is the yield, and what a sight: resin appears like caramel and the buds bulge.

Keep EC levels low, with regular (weekly) flushing and a two-week flush to finish to give the best results. Shiva has good resistance to mold and can tolerate 75% relative humidity. Outdoor/greenhouse growers will enjoy this strain with its good resistance, short flower cycle, and excellent returns of gourmet herb as a single stem, tied down producing forearms for colas, although heed Shiva Skunk's onset growth frenzy, particularly with a long vegetation cycle.

AROMA, TASTE AND EFFECT

A complex aroma that has a noticeable 'perfumed' tone to it. When cutting the bud there is a strong fruity aroma—apples, pears and peach cocktail laced with a musk that is quite unique and very appealing. The taste transitions superbly, carrying the musky fruit flavor over the palate and reminding me of Indian temples and the incense fragrance that shrouds them...truly mystical. If Shiva Skunk is allowed to flower to start of week eight and dried over four weeks in the dark, the effect is mind-folding. The hit from a eight-week bud is medicinal strength, inducing a trippy state of mind. This is a very potent herb that can only be fully appreciated during free time. Shiva Skunk delivers to head and body and is excellent for deep, long conversations; to unwind with; or for evenings in. The length of effect is extensive and the taper off unnoticeable with no ceiling level. This is a truly spiritual herb.

CURED BUD

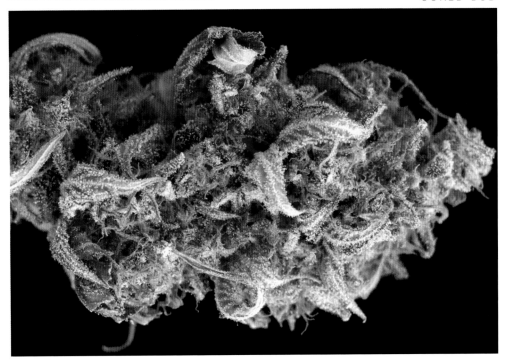

CURED BUD/CLOSEUP

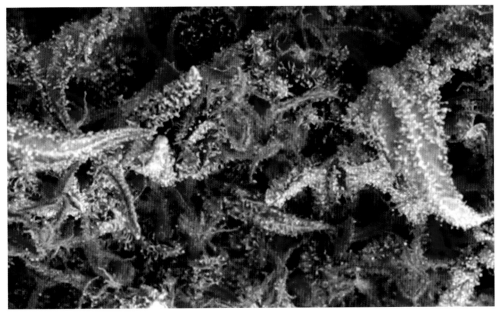

SUPER SILVER HAZE

FLOWER PERIOD: 84-91 days
APPROX. FINISHED ON-SET HEIGHT: 80-100%
MAXIMUM RELATIVE HUMIDITY: 80%

MAXIMUM TDS / EC: 1.4 / CF: 14 / PPM: 980
3 x 400 WATT x 25cm POT / YIELD = 100gms+

This strain grows with typical Sativa/Haze structure at a moderate pace, producing staggered nodal points off the main stem. Tipping encourages growth from the lower laterals and opens the format up slightly. For a large plant allow Super Silver Haze to reach 50-60cm before inducing onset as a gain of approximately 80-100% can be expected. Super Silver Haze's upper laterals do not open out like a typical Haze format, instead growing vertical and parallel (tower format); only 'budding up' forces them to open slightly. Multiple single stem setups would only need to get clones rooted and between 4-7 days in main set up or approximately 15-20cm to induce onset. Thirty-two single stems in a large 90cm2 Flood 'n' Drain hydro setup is an excellent way of maximizing the yield from a plant, with long flower cycle.

At nine weeks of flowering the buds are soft and fluffy with white stigmas, large but with no density yet. Keep EC levels low and flush regularly, from 63 days flush to the finish. There are no leaves, they having died off with the long duration; simply snip the buds straight into jars. This strain has excellent resistance to mold, tolerating relative humidity of 80%. If environmental control is not possible, keep a watchful eye for dying leaves and remove immediately. Super Silver Haze finishes slightly shorter than most Sativa-dominant crosses and is more compact. It is an extremely exciting strain to grow and though 12-13 weeks is a haul, to witness the baseball bats developing weekly is anxiety-building of the highest level and premium gourmet herb must be on hand to allow this epitome of plants to run its course of hardening and resin production. A grower can feel humbled in the presence of a mighty Super Silver Haze at 91 days.

Outdoor/greenhouse growers should excel with this variety although be sure to monitor humidity toward the end of season due to the extended flowering time needed to properly finish Super Silver Haze. Tipping, tying down, or preferably both keeps plants out of sight and increases yield factor. It is possible for indoor growers to finish earlier, possibly by the 70 days, and that is done by winding down the hours from 42 days by 30 minutes per week until 10-hour light periods are reached, and keeping this cycle to the finish. Observe for any hermaphroditing as light shortening can freak out Sativa-dominant plants. I prefer to run Super Silver Haze to 91 days. This is a very versatile strain that guarantees the finest premium herb available and for me Super Silver Haze is the top echelon a grower can achieve.

AROMA, TASTE AND EFFECT

The long wait now over, a four-week dry in the dark releases a strong citrus lime fragrance upon cutting into the bud. The taste is quite different, with an intoxicating flavor of ammonia! The burn off permeates the air as the palate is literally awash with this ammonia tasting experience which must be 'acquired' over two or three tokes (cones) for those accustomed to floral/fruity flavors. The smoke is as smooth as cognac, no coughing after cones, which replicate the flavor sensation, as well as spliffs. The effect is comparable to stepping into a hot bath in winter, soothing the mind and cradling the body, taking the toker to many different levels. Try indulging in a couple of cones with coffee after breakfast on a day off, as the duration is very prolonged, as you would hope. This is in a class of its own: for growers seeking the 'old high' of the '70s 'strength and length,' this is the one!

BUBBLE HASH

This would probably be one of the most significant revolutionary steps the industry has taken, in that every home grower with the bag system can produce top quality hash from different parts of the plant using trim, lower fluffy buds, and leaf to bud. Herb that has been lost to mold can be used for hash as oil does not mold.

Simply using ice and a sifting process through fine mesh screens at the base of the bags produces grades of hash, the final grade being the primo and usually the least quantity of the grades. Bubble hash is so clean of contaminants (fine plant matter) that if put to a flame as with traditional hashish, bubble hash will melt. The only difference that is noticeable is the consistent flavor, regardless of strain, of hash without any of the individual aromas and tastes that are present in traditional hand-sifting methods. I have no answer to this situation. Nevertheless, Bubble hash does have a very distinctive taste and aroma that will have your mouth watering and demanding to toke it.

Bubble hash is best left to dry naturally over…as long as you can hold out, up to two weeks, turning it over daily to encourage even drying in a dark drawer/room.

Bubble hash is very strong. Remember, it is the glands you are after, so whether they come from bud or leaf they will be strong (length of flower cycle is critical to potency).

Prepare herb by chopping bud up to roughly half the size of a match head, as when the pieces get wet and worked they open up. Approximately 200gms of dried bud can be used for each application. Snap freeze prepared herb for one to two hours prior to rinse as this helps glands to come away immediately.

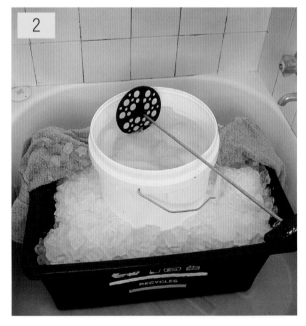

Place a 20-liter bucket 2/3 full of water into a bowl/ reservoir and pack with ice, wrapping a towel completely around the container of ice and the neck of bucket to retain temperature. Use purchased ice for convenience, ensuring its drinking quality, and pour ice into water (pre-chilling the water in a fridge the night before helps for a quick start) leaving approximately 10cms from the top to allow for vigorous movement in the bucket. Wait for temperature to read 1°C as this is minimum temperature required for gland removal.

Place snap-chilled material into bucket and stir in for approximately 10-15 minutes, changing directions and agitating. A paint stirrer as used in this demo is very good as you keep the head at the base of the bucket and using elliptical rotations to half the depth before rotating the head back down again, prevent the head coming too near the surface, as it pushes a bow of water ahead of it that may cause spillage. Reverse the direction periodically and be smooth and rhythmical with the action, no need for aggressive turning as the elliptical movement brings everything from the bottom up. Work for 10-15 minutes and then let stand for 20-30 minutes, repeating three more times. A paint paddle with a drill attachment can be used but keep speed to a minimum.

When complete, place first bag (color coded—read kit instructions) in order of rotation, into an empty 20l bucket and pour the finished mix into the bag slowly. This bag allows all resin glands of all sizes through its screen, plus extremely fine matter.

Slowly lift bag out, allowing several minutes to drain, then gently squeeze excess out and place bag with ice and 'matter' into an empty bucket. This matter can be saved and rinsed again or disposed of.

The dark-colored water can now be poured into a second bucket containing the second of the graded bags.

Pour contents into bag carefully. Do not rush and pour it off the sides so as to prevent glands being forced through the mesh at the base.

Use a prop to tie bag onto. Place a bucket underneath. After the water has passed through the bag, the bucket beneath will be quite full.

When all the water has almost passed through the bags, the hash can be seen clearly on the mesh screen. Use a plant mister to spray through the screen and the hash runs to the bottom of the bag forming a nice bulge.

Lay bag on a table and fold the base in half, folding the hash over itself. Using coffee filters press very gently through the bag, pressing the water out of the slab. After using four to five filters open bag, fight off the intoxicating aroma of hash and lift the slab out, turning the bag inside out to free little bits here and there on the mesh. It should be pressed a few times to remove excess moisture to speed up drying, then left to dry naturally. Obviously potency is as good as the stage trichomes were allowed to reach in flower. Peak potency produces a really potent product. One cone of a 'green and bubble' cocktail is extremely distorting.

SUPER SKUNK

FLOWER PERIOD: 49-56 days
APPROX. FINISHED ON-SET HEIGHT: 100-130%
MAXIMUM RELATIVE HUMIDITY: 75%

MAXIMUM TDS / EC: 1.4 / CF: 14 / PPM: 980
3 x 400 WATT x 25cm POT / YIELD = 90gms+

This is a classic hardy plant that grows at a fast pace with classic long ladyfinger leaves producing many distanced, staggered nodal points off the main stem that will give the plant a very broad, open structure with laterals having lots of space to develop and profuse secondary growth giving a big plant a very busy, congested appearance. Super Skunk is an excellent variety for multiple single stem setups, after rooting requiring 4-7 days or approximately 15-20cm in the main flowering room before inducing onset. A very powerful 'skunk' aroma permanently surrounds these plants, so odorless extraction filters are a necessity. In large plant setups, allow Super Skunk to reach 25-30cm to ensure a high number of laterals. Due to profuse development after maturity, Super Skunk can be grown as a large single stem facilitated by tying down at an early stage. With an extended vegetation cycle it will return excessive yields by start of week eight. However, for a standard large indoor example, inducing onset at approximately 50-60cm will result in an overall gain of approximately 100-130%. It has a quick response time and by start of week five resin production is under way, along with hardening.

Good resistance to mold, tolerating relative humidity of 75% and possibly a few digits higher, although if no environmental control is possible, observe for dying leaves and remove immediately. Such is the size of the colas, they are capable of exceeding the size of a forearm, producing very highcalyx-to-leaf, gourmet herb. At 49 days the buds are very swollen and resin coverage is good with the strong telltale aroma. If allowed to finish at 56 days there is a noticeable yield increase and a much heavier coating of resin. I really enjoy growing Super Skunk and always have a copy in my 'personals.'

Keep EC levels low, flushing weekly, ensuring a two-week flush to finish for the authentic taste. Outdoor/greenhouse growers should have very good success with Super Skunk's short flower cycle; this gives the grower a finished plant in the case of having to prematurely harvest, before seasonal change. The extended vegetation cycle will require Super Skunk to be tied down, keeping the plant hidden, and secondary budding sites will thus get maximum sunlight as laterals will be horizontal. At finish the plant can resemble a carpet of colas and excessively large buds (depending on grower's experience). Be aware of the strong fragrance in the last weeks of flowering; if possible use highly scented plants (roses, jasmine) to help mask the aroma and at all costs, do not disturb buds during final weeks of flower. This is a high calyx to leaf product, requiring very little manicuring after drying, with a fabulous, skunky aroma that is so familiar and established. Super Skunk consistently produces high quality returns of gourmet herb.

AROMA, TASTE AND EFFECT

When cut a powerful aroma of extreme skunk hits the nose. The aroma is for me a powerful blend of ripe mangos and ripe pineapple on the high note. The taste transitions extremely well and the palate feels like it has been refreshed by a mouthwash, overriding any lingering flavors prior to this indulgence. The flavor remains remarkably distinct for some time after indulging, be careful who you breathe on! This one is tops after breakfast with coffee to start the day; the duration is long with a taper off that is unnoticeable. This is a real productive smoke that is very euphoric and uplifting and really excels as a wonderful daytime indulgence.

SWEET TOOTH #4

FLOWER PERIOD: 49-56 days
APPROX. FINISHED ON-SET HEIGHT: 50-75%
MAXIMUM RELATIVE HUMIDITY: 75%

MAXIMUM TDS / EC: 1.4 / CF: 14 / PPM: 980
3 x 600 WATT x 25cm POT / YIELD = 130gms+

This is an Indica plant with leaf stems like rhubarb inherited from the Blueberry parentage. A slow-paced grower to begin, it produces many closely staggered nodal points off the main stem ensuring a high number of laterals later in life or if tipped. Leaves are dark green with a blue shimmer and extensively large; trimming across width of some leaves removing 50% will be required to facilitate with light getting to otherwise hidden buds. If tipping for a large plant, wait till approximately 25cm. Sweet Tooth #4's slow growth and nodal structure will facilitate an abundance of strong laterals that will remain tightly clustered to the main stem until maturity moves them away from center but still predominantly growing parallel and vertical.

Ensure a good size is reached for large plant setups, approximately 50-60cm before inducing onset as expect an overall gain of approximately 50-75%. Multiple single stem setups would require extra vegetation time after rooting, inducing onset at approximately 20-25cm. Keep EC levels low and flush regularly ensuring a two-week flush to finish. It has excellent resistance to mold and can tolerate relative humidity up to 75%, although the buds are so dense, be sure to watch for dead/dying leaves and remove immediately.

Structured for the commercial market, with Sweet Tooth #4 personal growers have a great opportunity to purchase a top value variety with exceptional qualities and great versatility. Outdoors/greenhouse setups with extended vegetation cycle and tipping can produce miniature trees packed with gourmet bud. With a high calyx to leaf ratio and a quick finish it should stay ahead of seasonal change and aid with drying. Sweet Tooth #4 is ready at 49 days with the finished look of rock-hard buds with excellent resin coverage. Personal growers may want to harvest 56 days to squeeze out the complete finish with a noticeable increase in both these factors, plus a color spectrum that is captivating.

AROMA, TASTE AND EFFECT

A distinct berry aroma hits the nose but not as bold or earthy as that of a full Blueberry, more sweet. On the fringes lurks a skunky fragrance but kept well enough at bay not to impede the fruit but rather compliment it. When the herb is jarred or bagged the aroma erupts on opening like springing a zip-lock container of fresh fruit. The taste is 'berry' on the inhale, the exhale is 'berry' with slight undertones of skunk leaving the palate to savour a fine-tasting fruit. I take Sweet Tooth #4 to 56 days and allow a 4-week slow dry in the dark and the effect on smoking is of a heavy delivery to the head obliterating most 'post-toking' plans. The body relaxes for an extensive period of time, making this ideal at the end of the day or on evenings in. Storing Sweet Tooth #4 will increase the buds' blue hues.

CURED BUD

CURED BUD/CLOSEUP

SWEET TOOTH #3 X G13

FLOWER PERIOD: 56-63 days
APPROX. FINISHED ON-SET HEIGHT: 100-130%
MAXIMUM RELATIVE HUMIDITY: 80%

MAXIMUM TDS / EC: 1.4 / CF: 14 / PPM: 980
3 x 400 WATT x 25cm POT / YIELD = 85gms+

This strain grows at a fast pace from rooting, developing many widely staggered nodal points which translate to fewer laterals that move away from center, but not enough to resemble an open format, tending instead to grow more vertical and parallel with profuse secondary development. Through vegetation cycle it has a tower format until colas and buds force the limbs to open up a little. Leaves are medium-sized, Indica format with round serration and a liberal scattering of fans that die off toward the finish. Tipping will help to control height and encourage more lateral growth making for a fuller plant and an increased yield.

For a large indoor plant, allow Sweet Tooth #3 x G13 to reach 25-30cm before tipping, to ensure a high number of laterals. An option to this is to tie down (area permitting) for a substantial increase in yield. If grown as a big single stem simply tie down the travelling head regularly and allow laterals to mature before tying them off to allow secondaries to reposition and begin the vertical climb. For a short plant flower early, approximately 20-25cm height, and tip at the same time.

When onset is induced expect a mainly vertical gain of approximately 100-130%. Budding sites do have trouble keeping their closeness and end up being staggered; tying down offsets this occurrence and keeps budding sites close. The staggered budding sites up the stems finally lock up for a crown of great size; the golf ball nugs are everywhere and this is where the yield lies, in the many secondaries. This has excellent resistance to mold, tolerating relative humidity 80%. Keep EC levels low and flush regularly ensuring a two-week flush to finish. Resin production is fierce, very G13, and the leaves and buds have a distinct blue hue to them, from the Sweet Tooth line.

This is an excellent multiple single stem set-up variety, requiring little vegetation time after rooting, inducing onset at approximately 15-20cm and finished 63 days. Greenhouse/outdoor growers will excel with this variety using tie-down method with the extended vegetation cycle for excellent returns of sensational bud with a unique gourmet flavor. At start of week nine the golf balls have blue and purple hues that lie beneath a 'sheet' of resin and are super-dense. Aesthetically speaking, these are among the most enchanting buds I've been privileged to see and this variety is quite simply a jewel.

AROMA, TASTE AND EFFECT

The fragrance of the bud when cut is root beer with undertones of ginger, which transitions to taste superbly, a very refreshing flavor reminiscent of the soft drink. The effect is sedative and of long duration; a session on this strain will end in chronic couchlock, making it ideal if there are long gaps between tokes. Excellent for winding down to at the end of the day, this is gourmet quality herb with a unique flavor.

CURED BUD

THE SPLIFF

A well prepared spliff is vital to the enjoyment of the product. Learning to roll a perfect number or scoob takes patience and best of all, practice. I use King size rolling papers and specific roach card as printed card is a health hazard. Spliffs are the most decadent way of enjoying herb, due to the amount of herb required. Flavors are more pronounced than any other toking implement I have used. I have great interest with the varying shapes I see other people roll and their rolling method, its fascinating. One doob I shared had four chambers attached to the main dooby, each chamber had a different herb in, five herbs in total from one toke. After we finished I was in an awful state. When learning the craft remember, as long as you can create and toke an efficient device, the actual shape or style you desire will soon follow.

After selecting the variety, place into a cup or bowl and work on using scissors for a few minutes. Using preferably a King-Size skin, and the Blues in most varieties provide a lightweight paper, less is better and with no overlap aids the joint in slower burning.

The prepared mix should have a melt effect; by holding the cup/bowl on an angle run the blades of the scissors through the mix and you should see the mix slowly fold or melt back into the groove left by the blades.

In this case take a king-sized single paper and place the gum side to the bottom edge facing away from you. Place the mix into the skin. Pour the mix in roughly creating the shape you require.

Pick up the skin and in this procedure angle one end, and gently roll between your fingers using the thumb, index and middle finger. Keep the other end narrow as it will open a little after gumming. As the shape is made by rolling the paper to and fro, the gum edge comes round and begins the start of the overlap. Gently roll until the shape is formed.

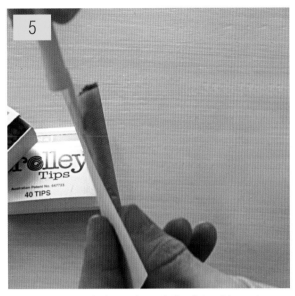

Ensure the gummed edge underneath lies flat and has not curled under. A pen lid can be used to simply resolve any problems with paper curl.

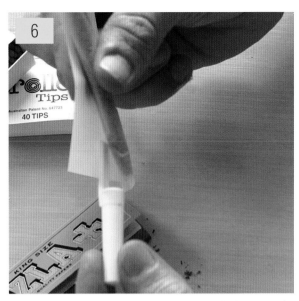

A pen lid or match can be used to untangle ravelled paper at the narrow roach end. This can be frustrating, creating an insertion point for the roach. Like all things, with a little diligence and practice the 'tangle' becomes less and easier to correct.

Hold at the overlap clearly visible and lick along the length of the gummed edge beneath the overlap; moisture moves through the top surface and onto the gummed edge below.

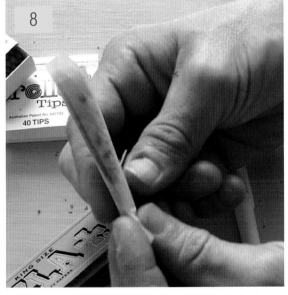

Smooth the overlap ensuring most of the gummed edge has been moistened and leave for a minute to adhere.

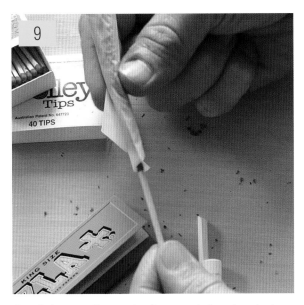

Open hole out gently, ensuring its access to the mix and not one of the overlaps, using a match. Gently (as it's only temporary) twist the filling end to prevent fallout while completing the job.

Use specifically made roach card, as it is clean and printed matter does not go under stringent rules for inhalation when used as a roach, so try to stick to this product. Roll up a length or, depending on the size of the roach hole, if necessary cut card in half for a thinner roach and roll tightly in both directions around a match. If too large for hole, re-roll without the match to get a thinner roach.

Roll-up roach.

Carefully insert roach into the hole.

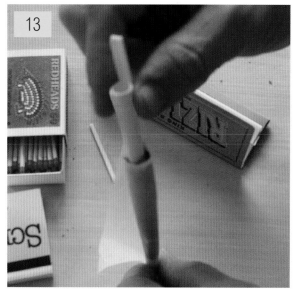

Re-open the end and top-up if necessary.

Twist the end to seal.

Pull the excess flap to one side.

Burn off the flap holding away from direction of flame. Some people lick the seal once more so the flame won't burn over the join and destroy the spliff.

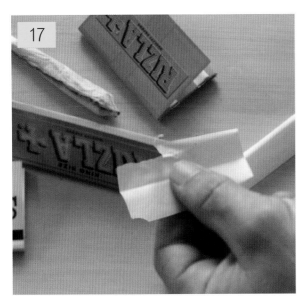

To ensure a good seal around roach and to facilitate a smooth, perfect toke, take one or two gummed edges from single papers.

Wrap round the join where start of roach meets the mix, helping to reinforce that area and seal the roach for an efficient consistent draw. A second piece of roach can be rolled and inserted into the existing roach hole to prevent debris coming down the roach when drawing or simply roll a piece of paper into a small ball and insert into roach hole.

Enjoy!

TANGO

FLOWER PERIOD: 56-63 days
APPROX. FINISHED ON-SET HEIGHT: 60-85%
MAXIMUM RELATIVE HUMIDITY: 80%

MAXIMUM TDS / EC: 1.4 / CF: 14 / PPM: 980
3 x 400 WATT x 25cm POT / YIELD = 90gms+

This is an exciting variety to grow in anticipation of the smoke, due to the name. It's a moderate-paced grower producing staggered nodal points ensuring a multi-limbed, open structure later in life or when tipped that move away from center with prolific secondary development giving a rather congested look to the format. For big plant setups, allow Tango to reach approximately 25-30cm before tipping to allow for a high number of laterals. Alternatively, take cuttings from a mother one week into onset to engage lateral growth immediately after striking, developing a multi-limbed, open format from the start. (Plant modelled was taken from a mother one week into onset. At approximately 35cm the plant was supercropped thoroughly and onset induced, the result being a short, fully developed, single stemmed example.) Budding sites are close but can become staggered through the modest growth surge at onset. Leaves are medium sized with a liberal scattering of fans that are light green throughout both cycles.

Keep EC levels low and flush regularly, ensuring a two-week flush to finish for optimum results. For large indoor plants, inducing onset at 50-60cm you can expect an overall gain of approximately 60-85%. Multiple single stem setups will require a little extra vegetation time, allowing cutting to reach 20-25cm before inducing onset.

Tango has excellent resistance to mold, tolerating relative humidity of 80%, although if this figure cannot be controlled observe for dying leaves and remove immediately. Responds to onset quickly and by 35 days stigmas turn pink, hardening and resin production is under way, and there are still three to four weeks to finish. The colas and buds are dense at 56 days and resin coverage is excellent, however both these factors undergo a noticeable increase if finished 63 days, to delivery premium quality, gourmet herb with a mule kick! Colas can exceed forearm-size with individual nugs resembling golf balls. For outdoor/greenhouse growers, this has to be one of the best-suited, as with the extended vegetation cycle, tipping and tying would return among the heaviest yields a plant is capable of—truly serious.

AROMA, TASTE AND EFFECT

Tango is another flavor sensation, with strong citrus aroma to the buds of orange, the parentage being of the orange family crossed with the mango. The taste is a bold, earthy strong orange that has real body to it; you could serve this on toast! The palate is left to savour a taste that reflects traditional Olde English marmalade; simply handling the bud sets the mouth into a watering frenzy. The effect is strong and sedative, better for the end of the day but as the duration of the effect is impressively prolonged and with no ceiling limit, it's ideal for long breaks between tokes (perish the thought). Try Tango before bed with a mug of hot chocolate.

CURED BUD

CURED BUD/CLOSEUP

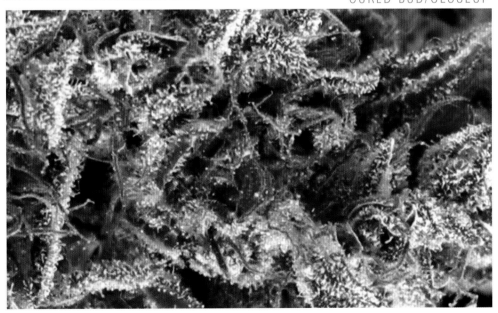

ULTIMATE INDICA

FLOWER PERIOD: 49-56 days
APPROX. FINISHED ON-SET HEIGHT: 50-70%
MAXIMUM RELATIVE HUMIDITY: 75%

MAXIMUM TDS / EC: 1.4 / CF: 14 / PPM: 980
3 x 600 WATT x 25cm POT / YIELD = 130gms+
MAXIMUM RESIN PRODUCTION AT 49 DAYS

Ultimate Indica is a slow-paced grower even when onset induced, developing closely staggered nodal points that ensure a prolific production of laterals later in life or if tipped. In large plant setups tip at 25-30cm to ensure a high number of laterals that very slowly move away from center but not enough to open the plant up like other Indicas, the plant remaining fairly compact in structure until bud weight forces laterals to open. For this variety to remain in vegetation stage it will require a 24-hour light cycle; laterals at the base of the plant stay very close to main stem forming a giant cola from the dirt up.

Keep EC Levels low and flush frequently to get the best product with a two-week flush to finish. For large plant setups, ensure a good-sized plant of approximately 50-60cm is achieved before inducing onset as a gain of approximately 50-70% can be expected. Multiple single stem setups will require extra vegetation time after rooting, allowing cutting to reach approximately 20-25cm before inducing onset. If 18-hour cycle is used, Ultimate Indica goes into pre-flowering mode, still growing, which accelerates response time dramatically to 12-hour. Some leaves tend to block light from secondaries, but rather than removing, cut offending leaves across their width, reducing the leaf by 50% of its size. Inducing onset starts the budding frenzy and the speed of development is astounding; at four weeks the heads are very large and fluffy and by 35 days hardening is well under way, as is resin production, and by 42 days it has a finished look with size increasing dramatically over the next seven days.

Excellent resistance to mold considering bud density, tolerating relative humidity of 75%. At 49 days the first signs of 'horning-up' appear, signaling Ultimate Indica's finish. Personal growers may want to finish 56 days for a modest yield increase just to ensure the absolute finish, but most noticeable are the colors through this period, which are spectacular.

Outdoors/greenhouse setups will have excellent returns with extended vegetation cycle and quick finish: Ultimate Indica can be harvested before the seasonal change, which also aids with drying. This variety's versatility, together with all other aspects, makes this a very viable investment.

AROMA, TASTE AND EFFECT

A very powerfully fruity aroma erupts from the bud as you cut it—a fruit cocktail of apples, pears and peaches…a complex mélange of fruit. The taste however is richly different: dried fruit, figs and dates leave the palate with an exotic aftertaste to savour. The effect is immediately cerebral, mixing thoughts with a bit of fog. Perspiration is quick to follow, and then the body begins to feel unsupported and relaxed. This 'lock-up' can last awhile with no ceiling level—it continually pops you up to the stratosphere with a very slow descent, making Ultimate Indica suitable for after work or evening indulgence.

CURED BUD

CURED BUD/CLOSEUP

WARLOCK

FLOWER PERIOD: 56-63 days
APPROX. FINISHED ON-SET HEIGHT: 80-100%
MAXIMUM RELATIVE HUMIDITY: 65%

MAXIMUM TDS / EC: 1.4 / CF: 14 / PPM: 980
3 x 600 WATT x 25cm POT / YIELD = 130gms+

This variety is a moderate-paced grower through vegetation period, producing staggered nodal points off the main stem that later in life, or if tipped, will produce fewer laterals that will move away from center opening the structure up and allowing light good access to the secondaries. There are very few leaves on this variety and what there are, are medium-sized with the odd fan here and there and dark green in color, which they remain to the finish. Tipping Warlock if growing indoors for a large plant at 25-30cm, will facilitate in a high number of laterals. For large plant setups inducing onset at 50-60cm, Warlock will gain approximately 80-100%. Tying down (optional) allows Warlock to reach maximum potential and offset height.

Multiple single stem setups would require little vegetation time after rooting, inducing onset at approximately 15-20cm. Warlock is susceptible to mold, therefore keep relative humidity below 65% up to start of week six, then reduce to below 60% if possible. Keep EC levels low and flush regularly ensuring a two week flush to finish for optimum results.

The buds are tightly staggered up the stems and laterals; from the midway point they lock up to form impressive high calyx to leaf colas. Resin production, along with hardening, begin 42 days and by 56 days Warlock is ready although home growers may want to harvest 63 days just to be sure. Outdoor/greenhouse growers would require an arid climate or environmental control due to Warlock's vulnerability to mold, although with extended vegetation cycle and tipping, tying down and a relatively short flower cycle will give

very pleasing results from a high quality product that consistently finishes with colas exceeding forearms, with fierce resin production and very little manicuring after a four-week dry in the dark.

AROMA, TASTE AND EFFECT

The aroma of the bud when cut is a strong fruity one of pineapple. The taste is richly different but still fruity. The palate is left to savour the taste of plums—sweet on the inhale, rich through the exhale, with hashy undertones; it is top stuff. The effect is cerebral, uplifting and outgoing. Excellent for focusing and achieving things throughout the day. Very euphoric with coffee after breakfast, with a prolonged duration and a slow taper off that is unnoticeable. For people on the move requiring good, dynamic social interaction, Warlock is supreme—a top daytime smoke.

CURED BUD

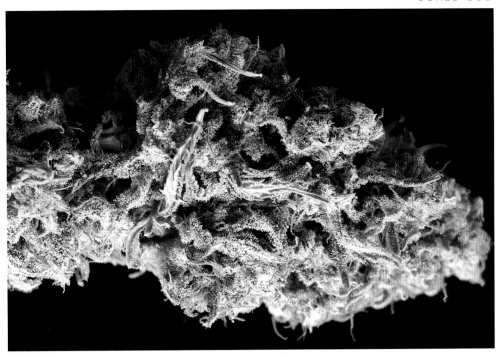

CURED BUD/CLOSEUP

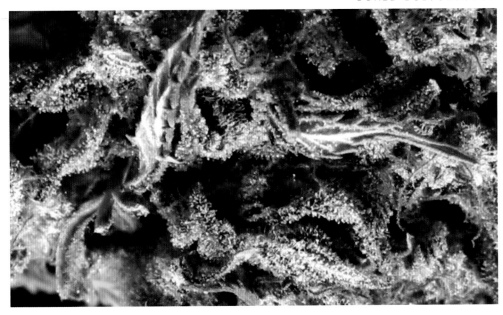

BONGS & VAPOURIZERS

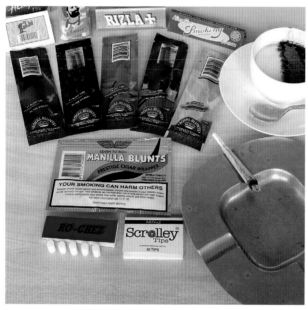

An array of paraphernalia—a multitude of papers, roaches and Blunt flavored cigar wraps for something completely different.

Enjoying herb, be it personally grown or purchased is specific to an individual. The preparation of herb regardless of delivery preference is a ritual: the selection, the testing, the filling of the bowl and the contemplation that takes place while preparing your mix dates back ritually through the ages. In addition to the spliff, discussed above, here are two popular means of delivery.

BONGS

Bongs are a serious accessory when it comes to toking and the style of the delivery is immediately overpowering for novices. One cone can debilitate and will alleviate any post-toke plans you may have had. There are so many versions in style and material, its

large following is understandable. The bong is an art piece, really, that always delivers.

I was introduced to a heaped cone on my first time, and would seriously recommend to other first-timers that they begin with only half a cone. Cones really belt you and three cones of primo herb will debilitate a spliffer.

Bongs are the heavyweight tool of this industry and have to be respected. Try to keep the body and stem clean with daily cleaning. Many citrus based shower products work well and fallen stems from pine trees work particularly well cleaning stem, discard after one clean. Cones can be scraped clean with a match stick after each toke.

VAPORIZERS

I personally use one and find it to be very effective. There are lots of types available and many do not actually vaporize; they combust, producing smoke. The temperature of the herb when toking is a crucial difference between vaporizing and combusting. Vaporizing produces a faint signature when exhaled that evaporates before traveling further than 12 inches, with no aroma. When removed the used herb should look unused in appearance but crumble when squeezed and have an aroma of popcorn.

If it's burnt in appearance the heat is too high. There are models available for chilling that actually push the vapor out of a mouthpiece using an electric motor so that the participants do not have to touch it, simply open wide and aim in! Herb goes even further using a standard vaporizing device than other techniques as so little is required.

No health risks is the big factor of this method with

Two popular styles of Bong L. Traditional bowl R. Pistol grip.

One of many Vaporizers with precut caps approximate size of match head for one delivery.

no discomfort making it the perfect device at parties and for first timers particularly if they do not smoke. The only drawback for me was lack of individual flavors. The flavor for me is consistent every time and it is hashy. Others that have adapted to this method may well have a different view and I accept that, but I could not have evaluated the varieties in the book using a vaporizer.

The effect is extremely euphoric and uplifting, and always cerebral for me regardless of the strain and amount. Its effect is immediate, within seconds your head feels light with a little spin to it. Certainly infrequent tokers (weekenders or nighttime only tokers)

would probably find this method heavier and sedative in quantity.

I find it a great device to have on hand and enjoy using it from time to time especially if I need to give my system a rest after a session.

WHITE WIDOW ORIGINAL

FLOWER PERIOD: 63-70 days
APPROX. FINISHED ON-SET HEIGHT: 100-130%+
MAXIMUM RELATIVE HUMIDITY: 80%

MAXIMUM TDS / EC: 1.4 / CF: 14 / PPM: 980
3 x 600 WATT x 25cm POT / YIELD = 160gms+

White Widow is a fast-paced grower after rooting, developing distanced staggered nodal points up the stem suggesting laterals will develop a broad, open structure. This will facilitate with light accessing the profuse development of secondaries, giving the plant a busy and congested appearance. Do not tip, as this will severely compromise White Widow's yield. It has to be tied down in large plant setups (do not be afraid), and after one or two crops you will be fully familiarized with the traits of White Widow and grow accordingly with consistent excessive returns. This model was tipped for research and produced 95gm. (The model prior was single stem tied down, approximately 25% larger plant and produced 185gm.)

For big plant setups allow White Widow to reach at least 50-60cm before inducing onset as a gain of approximately 100-130%+ can be expected. Laterals develop after plant is mature and established and these will require tying down and encourage new secondaries to begin the vertical climb. Multiple single stem setups will require little vegetation time after rooting, allowing cutting to reach approximately 15-20cm before inducing onset. In big plant setups, budding development is staggered but as growth slows, so they begin to stack to build an excessive cola on the center stem that can exceed calf size.

This plant responds to onset very quickly, with swollen buds and good resin coverage. Apart from the small size, White Widow has a finished look from 35 days, but resist! These heads literally grow by the week like air is being pumped into them. At 63 days White Widow is very acceptable, with excessive colas and excellent resin coverage, but incredibly, both these factors increase noticeably if the plant is allowed to run till 70 days. Excellent resistance to mold, tolerating maximum relative humidity of 80%, however such is the size and density of colas/buds, it would be wise to use control if possible.

Outdoor/greenhouse growers will excel with this strain that is capable of producing staggering returns with the long vegetation cycle and excellent mold resistance (though not impervious). Tying White Widow down will keep it hidden and the horizontal position will expose secondaries to unobstructed light (depending on grower's experience). The finished appearance can resemble a carpet of colas. Be aware that the aroma is very strong if handled or brushed against through flowering cycle, very 'skunky' indeed. White Widow is such a popular variety and one that will quickly become any grower's favorite, another true established classic.

AROMA, TASTE AND EFFECT

After coming to terms with the excessive returns comes the second wave of disbelief at White Widow's intoxicating aroma of cologne strength, an invigorating blend of tropical ripe mango, guava and passion fruit, laced with a full-bodied skunk influence. The fragrance is so rich, even seals on glass jars have trouble keeping this one at bay. It's impossible to keep even an unlit spliff from permeating the environment; this herb has to travel in glass. The taste transitions superbly well with the palate feeling like a mouthwash rinse, you can literally discard the toothbrush, several tokes is all it takes to replace sleep breath with a tropical zing. However the effect is debilitating—it is the .44 Magnum of herbs, delivering an immediate cerebral hit that in most cases will have a little moisture appearing around the eyes and forehead, and with the ability to come over the top of most other herbs. It is a heavy, deep state-of-mind hit and if not prepared to indulge in something, will have you sleeping. The duration is very prolonged, excellent if only a spliff or couple of cones need to last all day! Otherwise indulge in free time only to really allow White Widow the full effect. If stored, White Widow unbelievably improves, becoming even smoother. The flavor cannot be done justice by a description and the effect is trippy with no ceiling and an unnoticeable taper off.

CURED BUD

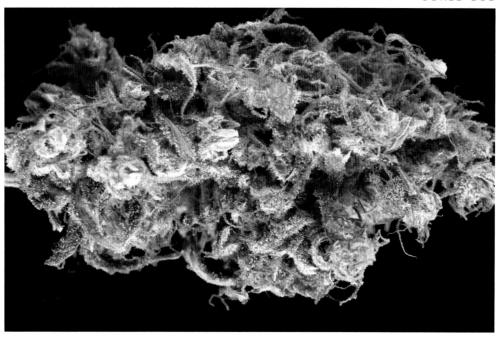

CURED BUD/CLOSEUP

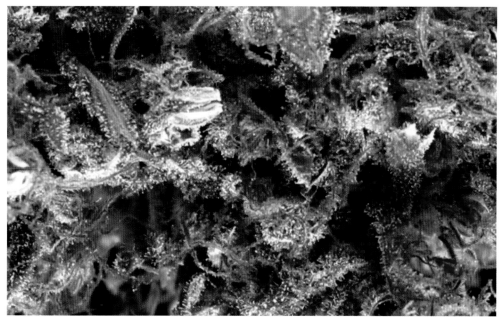

WHITE WIDOW #2

FLOWER PERIOD: 63-70 days
APPROX. FINISHED ON-SET HEIGHT: 100-130%+
MAXIMUM RELATIVE HUMIDITY: 80%

MAXIMUM TDS / EC: 1.4 / CF: 14 / PPM: 980
3 x 400 WATT x 25cm POT / YIELD = 95gms+

Another version White Widow from another seed bank, this is a fast-paced grower producing distanced staggered nodal points developing fewer laterals, that will grow and mature moving away from center to really open the plant out and facilitating with the profuse secondary development this strain produces, light having an unobstructed path to most budding sites. As we have seen above, White Widow must be grown as a single stem and tied, as tipping severely compromises yield. The leaves are large to fan-sized, but not too numerous, and the long ladyfinger blades are on extra-long stems allowing light to access budding sites. This model was taken from a mother seven days into onset, which encouraged profuse development of laterals immediately after rooting, giving the plant a very open format and still retaining a main center stem. Onset was induced at approximately 30-35cm and this coincided with one complete treatment of supercropping to offset growth surge through this period and substantially beef up cola size on such a short plant, as can be seen.

For large plant setups using tie down method, allow White Widow to reach approximately 50-60cm before inducing onset as a gain of approximately 100-130% can be expected. Multiple single stem setups will require little vegetation time after rooting, allowing cutting to reach approximately 15-20cm before inducing onset. Buds remain white and fluffy till 42 days, when resin production really gets underway, along with hardening, and these colas under 600-watt lighting get extremely dense. Coupled with a high calyx to leaf ratio, this makes for a very quick manicure after drying.

Keep EC levels low and flush weekly ensuring a two-week flush to finish. This strain shows excellent resistance to mold, tolerating a relative humidity of 80%. Outdoor/ greenhouse setups would also excel with White Widow, the long vegetation cycle and its favorable response to tying down should return excessive yields of premium grade herb that, hard to believe, will be more potent than the indoor version. White Widow can make most gardeners humble in awe of its yield.

AROMA, TASTE AND EFFECT

White Widow #2 has a strong citrus lemon aroma and when jarred gets a skunky fragrance on opening, but when cut the strong citrus lemon returns. The taste transitions well, leaving the palate with a refreshing lemon taste and with subtle skunky undertones. The effect is totally sedative: heavy head, fogged thoughts and relaxed in the body. It has a very prolonged effect with no ceiling level and an elevation on the taper off making it ideal at the end of the day and evenings in.

YUMBOLDT

FLOWER PERIOD: 56-63 days
APPROX. FINISHED ON-SET HEIGHT: 50-70%
MAXIMUM RELATIVE HUMIDITY: 70%

MAXIMUM TDS / EC: 1.4 / CF: 14 / PPM: 980
3 x 600 WATT x 25cm POT / YIELD = 130gms+

This strain is a slow grower producing closely staggered nodal points up the main stem that will produce a high number of laterals later in life or if tipped. Leaves are medium to large with a rounded serration and a liberal scattering of fans. Tipping encourages Yumbolt to open up and new laterals mature moving away from center with secondaries forming a complex framework within the structure. This model was tipped at approximately 25cm to facilitate growth of a high volume of laterals with time to mature.

For a large indoor version induce onset at approximately 50-60cm expecting an overall gain of approximately 50-70%. Budding sites remain closely staggered through this period, locking up toward the top of the stem for some mighty dense colas. Multiple single stem setups would require extra vegetation time after rooting, allowing cuttings to reach approximately 20-25cm before inducing onset.

Yumbolt has a very good resistance to mold, tolerating relative humidity of 70% and maybe higher. Outdoor/greenhouse setups will have excellent results with Yumbolt, tipping or tying-down with extended vegetation period will produce extremely pleasing trees. Yumbolt has a very high calyx to leaf ratio and development of buds/colas is very dense. At 56 days, Yumbolt can be harvested with very good resin coverage. Personal growers have the option to harvest at 63 days and it is worth seven days' wait as there is a noticeable increase in yield and resin. Use low EC levels, flushing weekly, ensuring a two-week flush to finish for optimum results. This is an excellent purchase in any setup that is guaranteed to please, with the significant factor of virtually no manicuring after drying four weeks in the dark! Pucker.

AROMA, TASTE AND EFFECT

Yumbolt is a real fruity cocktail of apples, pears and pineapple…very appealing. The taste is unmistakably one of plum that departs with the exhale leaving a hashy aftertaste to savour. The effect is sedative with an immediate cerebral delivery and the body relaxing soon after over an extensive period of time. Yumbolt is a very powerful herb with no ceiling that encourages creative thinking; excellent at the end of the day. This copy was purchased from the original seed bank carrying Yumbolt.

CURED BUD

CURED BUD/CLOSEUP

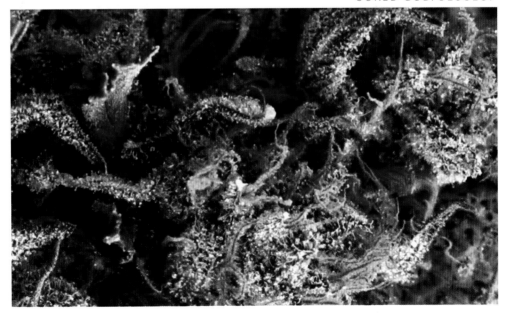

CUTTING GALLERY

Bubblegum #1 seedling

Bubblegum #2 seedling

Caramella seedling

Mazar i-Shariff Seedling

Shiva Skunk Seedling

American Dream cutting taken from mother 1 week into on-set

Bubblegum #2 cutting taken from mother 1 week into on-set

Cinderella 99 cutting taken from mother 1 week into on-set

Chronic cutting taken from mother 1 week into on-set

Leda Uno cutting taken from mother 1 week into on-set

Yumbolt cutting taken from mother 1 week into on-set

Ultimate Indica cutting taken froma mother on 24 hour 'lights-on' cycle.